# INSPIRATIONAL WISDOM

### A Collection

*Thoughts, contemplation and the Realities of Life*

## LORNA RAMIREZ

# The Realities of Life

## My Innermost Thoughts

Lorna Ramirez

Published in Australia by Lorna Ramirez
This edition published 2021

Copyright © Lorna Ramirez 2021

Cover design, typesetting: Chameleon Print Design

The right of Lorna Ramirez to be identified as the Author of the Work has been asserted in accordance with the Copyright, Designs and Patents Act 1988.

All rights reserved. No part of this publication may be reproduced, stored in a retrieval system, or transmitted, in any form or by any means without the prior written permission of the publisher, nor be otherwise circulated in any form of binding or cover other than that in which it is published and without a similar condition being imposed on the subsequent purchaser.

Ramirez, Lorna
Inspirational Wisdom

ISBN:
Paperback: 978-0-6482130-8-6
Ebook: 978-0-6482130-9-3
pp466

# Table of Contents

My Innermost Thoughts (The Realities of Life)
    About the author      ix
    Acknowlegements      xi
    Dedication      xiii
    Preface      1
    My Poems      3
    My Inner Thoughts      35
    My Wisdoms      103

Reflective Contemplations      173
    Acknowledgements      175
    Preface      179
    A. Contemplations      181
    B. Reflections      251

Pondering Thoughts
    Acknowledgements      295
    1. Human and Divine Love      299
    2. Perfect Imperfection      302
    3. Pondering Thoughts      305
    4. Winter Season in Our Lives      308
    5. The Wheel Of Life      311

| | |
|---|---:|
| 6. A Christmas Story (True Story) | 314 |
| 7. Life Begins at "Any Age" | 318 |
| 8. Spring of Life | 321 |
| 9. Worlds Apart | 324 |
| 10. Is it Fate or Destiny? | 328 |
| 11. For the Love of God | 332 |
| 12. The Most Beautiful Face on Earth | 335 |
| 13. Thanks for the Memories | 339 |
| 14. The Many Faces of Happiness | 342 |
| 15,. Chrysalis My Journey as an Author | 346 |
| Inspirational Messages and Thoughts | 353 |

My Passion, My Calling

| | |
|---|---:|
| Poems | 357 |
| Inspirational Messages | 391 |

# The Realities of Life

## My Innermost Thoughts

Lorna Ramirez

## About the Author

Lorna Ramirez is a writer, published author of five books, My Innermost Thoughts, My Passion, My Calling, Moments of Love, Lust and Ecstasy, Reflective Contemplations and Pondering Thoughts. She is also a publisher, motivational speaker, ghost writer a pianist and a regular contributor of The Philippine Times and the Sydney Philippine Community Herald.

She finished her Chemical Engineering degree at the University of Santo Thomas, Philippines and had worked as a Laboratory and Mill Manager at a Textile industry Philippines. Lorna has travelled extensively, gaining much from her interactions with people all over the world and building strong foundations for her philosophies in life. She loves gardening, cooking, reading and playing the piano both classical and modern.

In 1977 with her husband and her son and daughter she migrated to Australia. She worked as an Industrial Chemist in one of the leading oil companies in Australia, only retiring in the year 2000 to care for her first grandchild.

Lorna Ramirez won third prize for the 2017 writing competition by the Society of Women writers in Victoria. In October 2016 Lorna was one of the certificate of recognition award recipients from FILCCA ( Filipino Community Council of Australia) Lorna was voted one of the five Most Inspiring Woman of Australia in 2019 by The women's Association Incorporated. In 2020 she was recognised as one of the two Most Inspiring Women by the Skylark Foundation Australia.

Lorna is a founding member of the newly peak body CAFOVI (Council of Australian Filipino Organizations of Victoria) and also an active member of the Historical Society of Footscray.

She is a financial supporter of different charities, National Breast Cancer Foundation and Soriano-Orodio Foundation Inc. Australia The proceeds of her fourth book Reflective Contemplations were donated to this charity, the National Breast Cancer Foundation and to the different Church dioceses in the western suburb Victoria. She is also a financial -supporter for Mental Health Foundation, and Give Love Inc.

At present she is writing two books, one book she is writing, is a sequel of her novel Moments of Love, Lust and Ecstasy, and another book for inspirational messages, original poems and quotes.

She often also been invited to different libraries in Victoria to speak about writing and encouraging especially young would be writers, how to publish their written manuscript.

Throughout her life Lorna Ramirez a woman of faith, has been a wise observer of human behaviour and has collected her many wisdoms and observations to produce an inspiring and uplifting books.

# Acknowledgements

**My special thanks to**
Marie Franze
Renalyn Cerezo

for helping me to make my dream of publishing a book of my own a reality.

**To**
My loving husband, Claro
My grandkids, Alyssa and Amelia
My children and their partners –
Carlo and Marie
Maritess and Steve

# Preface

Any similarities to others' writings are coincidental. This is my original work.

My love and strong bonding with my family, my relationship with friends and extended family and my strong connection with God have inspired me.

I have explored my innermost feelings and offer my perspective on many aspects of life.

As I have matured my perceptions have changed because of my life's experiences and knowledge gained. I want to share the convictions and beliefs, value system and philosophies developed throughout my life.

My hope is that my innermost thoughts will touch and inspire you in some way.

**Lorna Ramirez**

# My Poems

## 1. EACH TIME

Each time, we breathe to live
Each time, we should remember that life is a gamble
Each time is a challenge
Each time is a journey because no one knows what the future brings and holds
Yes, we can try to plan and control our lives
But much to our dismay, we soon discover we can only do it to a certain degree
So as not to be bitterly disappointed, accept the things you cannot change
If you can change things, do them better next time
Indeed, these are the realities of life

The Realities of Life | Lorna Ramirez

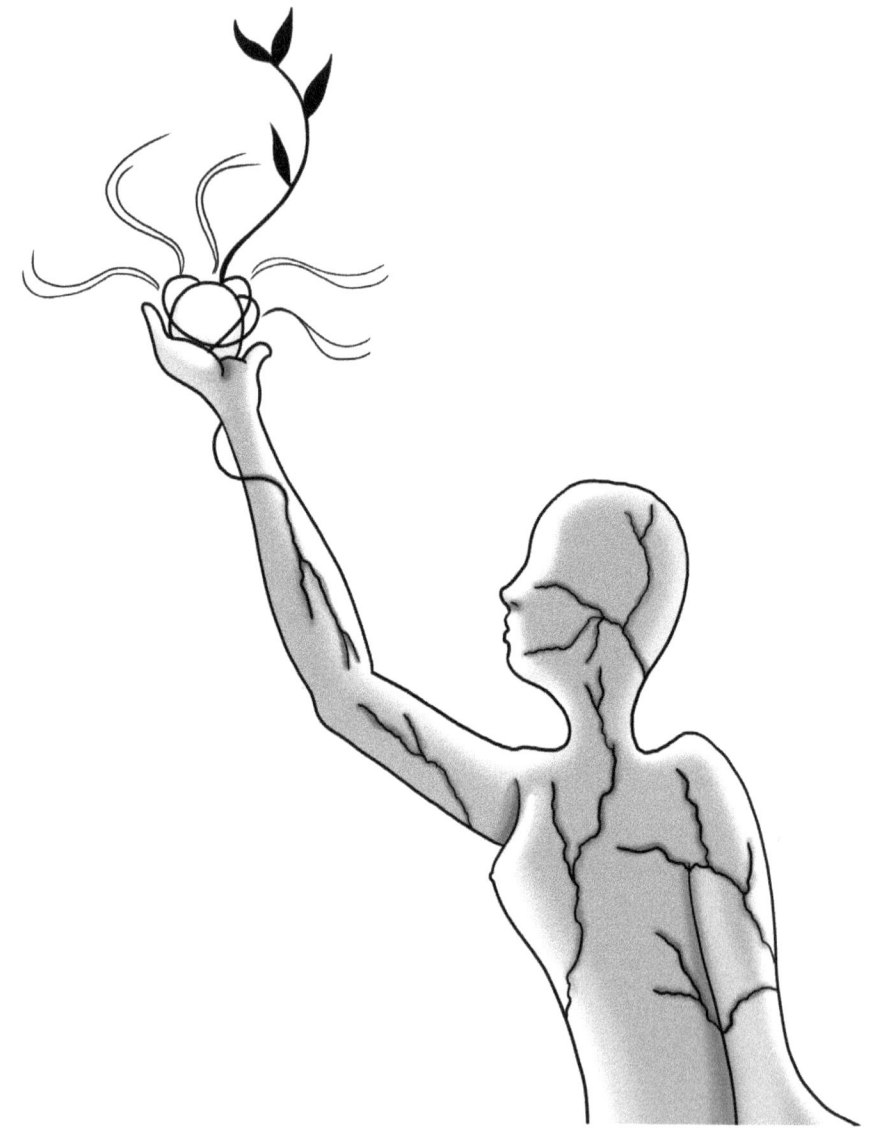

## 2. SUFFERING IN SILENCE

At times we cry within
Yet no one can hear
The pain and hurt, only you can feel
Those shattered dreams and memories of yester-years that
haunt you vividly as only they can
But that was then and today is different
Years have passed and things have changed
Once again, triumphantly, you emerge now
A better, stronger person

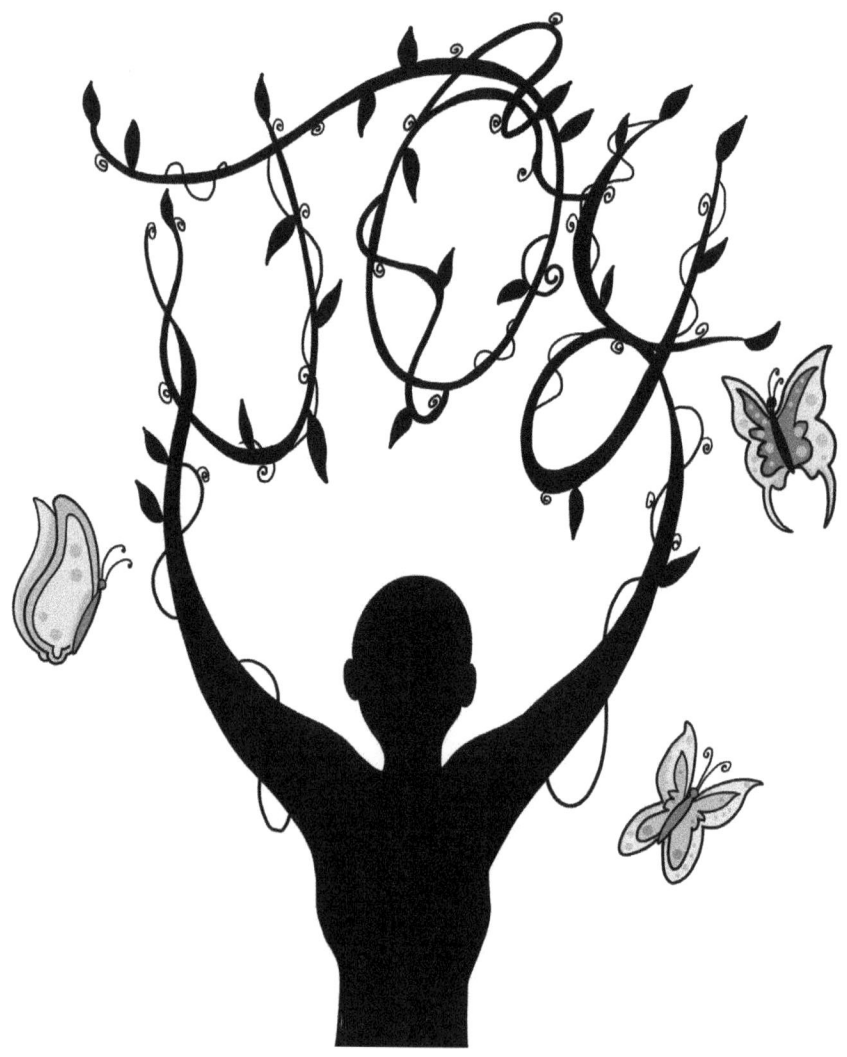

### 3. LOVING YOUR LIFE

Love the life you live
Appreciate the things you have
Be it small or big, wake up each day with enthusiasm
Full of hope and determination that today will be
Better than yesterday
Make tomorrow another day of joy and bliss

## 4. OUR GIFT TO MANKIND

It is with giving that we find the joy of sharing
It is in loving that we can fully feel how it is to be loved
It is in understanding that we can practise the art of compassion
It is by believing in ourselves that we can focus and do
anything our hearts desire
And most importantly
It is in trusting and believing in Him
That we can find all the inspiration and courage to do these things

## 5. A MOTHER'S LOVE

Giving without expecting in return
Loving with all thy heart no matter what
Understanding when others fail to understand
Supporting in times of sorrow and grief
Most of all,
Always being there for thy children in every way

The Realities of Life | Lorna Ramirez

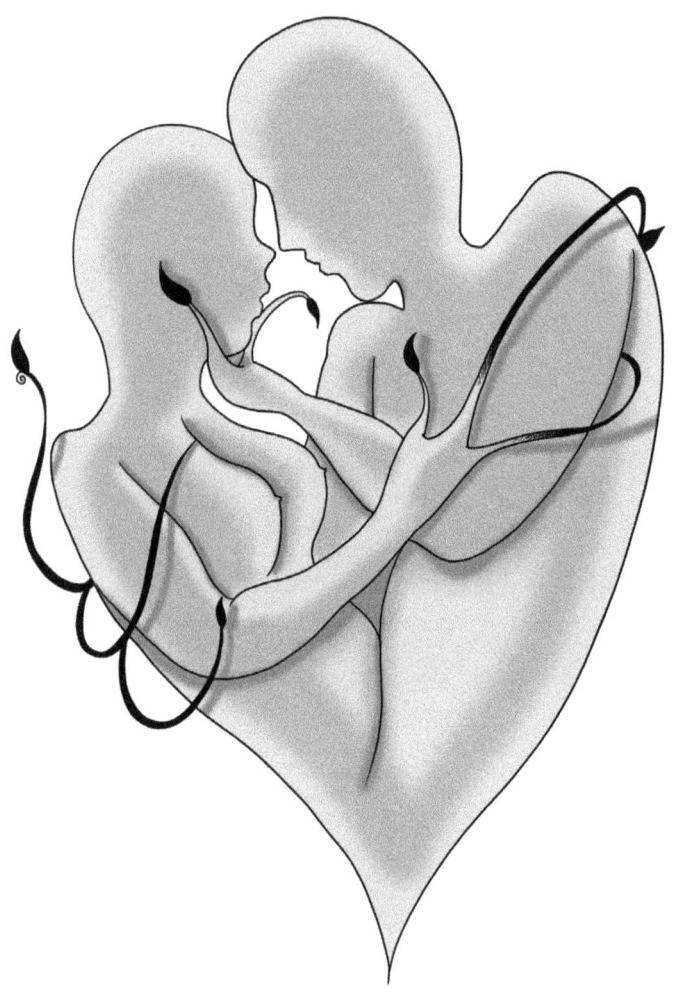

## 6. DEDICATED TO ALL HUSBANDS

He may not have the same thick curly hair
He may not have the lean physique
He may not have the same smooth baby-face look
But there are things that remain unchanged
He still has that cheeky smile
Same facial expression when angry, sad or happy
Still has the same sense of humour
Through the years he has always been
My mentor, my rock, my guide, my fiercest critic
But most of all, my real best friend
Like others, we have our highs and lows
But because of our love and support for each other We have
managed to go through each trial and triumph
If given the chance to do it over again
Without hesitation, I would do so,
With no regrets

## 7. NEVER

Never lose hope without fighting
Never give up without even trying
Never stop loving; it's the reason for living
Never stop believing in yourself
It's the secret of success
Never stop trusting Him
He will always know what is best for us

## 8. IT DOES NOT MATTER

It does not matter what they say
It does not matter what they think of you
It does not matter how they judge you
What matters most is being happy
Happy for the things you do
And believing in yourself

## 9. PRAISE THY LORD

Thank thee, Oh Lord
For all the wisdom
Bestowed upon me
For all the thoughts and words
That inspire me to write
If this is just a tool and way
For me to reach others
Console those who need the most
I am happy to do so
I know you will always be here
In my heart, mind and soul

## 10. PERSEVERANCE

In times of troubles
We sometimes question
Our very own existence
In times of mourning
We can find solace
In the arms of our loved ones
The past can be forgotten
But there are moments
The memories still haunt us
No matter how painful it was
We have to accept things as they are
Learn to move on
Tomorrow will be another day
Another day, hopefully
Of happiness and contentment

## 11. NEVER STOP

Never stop learning
Never stop stimulating your brain
Never stop believing in yourself
Never stop following your dreams
Never stop doing things
You are passionate about
Continually challenge yourself
Setting up goals to be an achiever
After all, life is too short
To be wasting your precious time

The Realities of Life  |  Lorna Ramirez

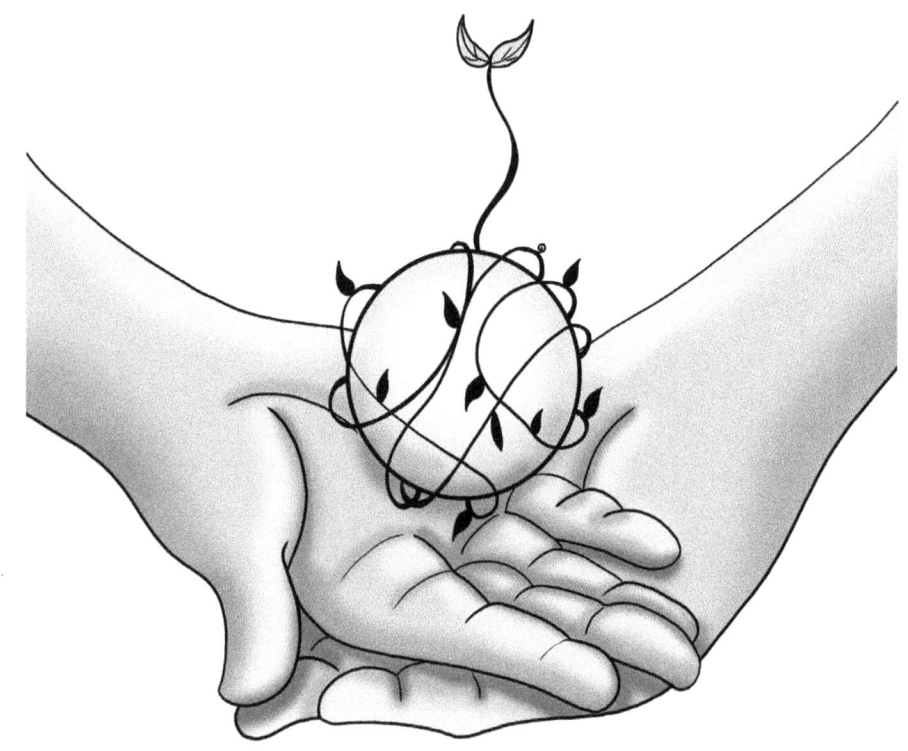

## 12. SPECIAL MOMENTS

Each special moment
Has that special meaning
That will be forever
Embedded in our hearts
Each challenge and endeavour
We have gone through
Needs patience, hope and perseverance
From each failure and mistake we have made
Lessons can be learned
Can be used as an inspiration
To start all over again
Till we have achieved our dreams.

## 13. GRANDCHILDREN

Grandchildren are sheer joy to have
Rekindled fun memories
Of the kids we once had
They bring happiness to the next phase of our lives
Now that we are in
The twilight years of our lives
We cannot get enough of them
All those special moments shared
It brings back our youth
The energy, zest and vigour we once had
And we thought we had lost

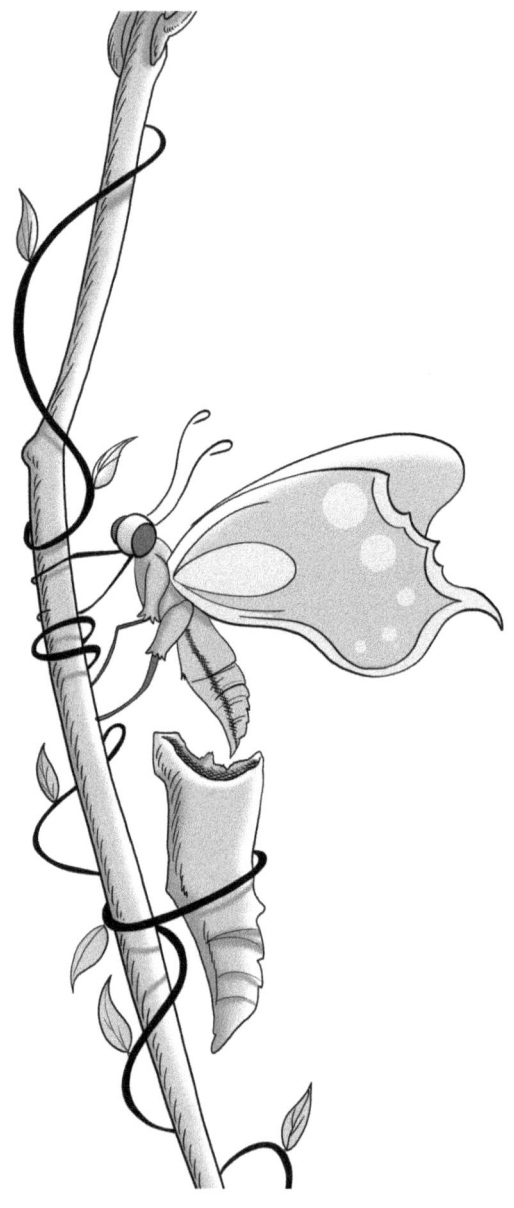

## 14. CHANGE

Change means courage, discipline
Change means humility
Acceptance of your fault and inadequacies
Change means enlightenment
The truth revealed
Change means aspiring
To do the right things at the right time
Take one step at a time.
With sheer determination
You can be a better person
Than you are now

The Realities of Life | Lorna Ramirez

## 15. LOVE (ACCEPTANCE)

It's easy to love the lovable
It's easy to accept people
Who share our beliefs and convictions
It's easy to love families and friends
It will take courage for us
To love and accept people
Who are different, unlovable
This world would be a peaceful place
If we tried to accept and respect everyone
Regardless of gender, race or religion
And other differences

The Realities of Life | Lorna Ramirez

## 16. MY FAITH IN GOD

With every quest I went through
With every trial I endured
With every frustration I had
With every fall I suffered
Without a doubt in my mind
I was able to go through all these
Because I knew that all these times
God would guide me and help me
Find the right way
And the right path to cross

# My Inner Thoughts

### 1. I BELIEVE

Whenever there is Hope, inner strength will follow
Whenever there is Love, compassion will prevail
Whenever there is Struggle, solutions will be near and it will finally come to an end
Whenever there is Doubt, one day you will find the light
These are only a few of the many things that will cross our paths
And our strong belief and trust in Him will help us overcome
All the difficulties we can encounter at any time in our lives

## 2. THANKSGIVING

Never a day passes that I don't thank Him for all the blessings
I have
For the moment I wake up each day pain-free and still full
of energy
Able to do things that I am passionate about
Being grateful and feeling blessed having such a caring,
wonderful family, relations and friends
When the time comes, I will be able to face Him proudly and
I will be able to say
Though I have not amassed great fortune and fame
I have done my part well as a mother, wife and friend
At peace with everybody
And always connected to Thee

## 3. ANGER

There are times we can equate Anger to Pain
Some are angry because they feel the pain of being abused, neglected, frustrated and betrayed
Whatever the reasons may be
One should always be strong and use the anger to fight back and overcome
Be focused to succeed and conquer the pain you feel

## 4. SPIRITUAL UPLIFTMENT

If the food we take nourishes our body
Prayers, meditations and contemplations are the tools
enriching and uplifting our spiritual souls
Through these we grow to control our minds and emotions
Thus bringing us to the next level where inner peace and
satisfaction can easily be achieved

## 5. NEVER STOP

Once you stop dreaming
Once you stop doing things you are passionate about
Stop making goals and stop being focused
You stop living
These are our inspirations and motivations
To wake up each day
Embrace the present with open arms and with the anticipation
That you will make the day better than yesterday
And tomorrow will be another day of challenge

## 6. THE PRICE OF FAME

At times a person is consumed by their success
They start to detach themselves with the real world
Even neglecting their loved ones and friends
It's sad; a high price to pay for fame

**7.**

All of us have gone through several stages in life
Each stage is a learning experience
At the end it's nice to look back
Not counting the years you have gone through
But counting the special moments
That you had been through

**8.**

Open your heart to those who need the most
Help and comfort to those who are grieving, confused
and disillusioned
At times like this they needed someone to cling to
Your support can at least ease the burden that they are carrying
At times like this, friendship will be put to the test
Lucky are those who have faithful friends and loving families
To support them in their darkest moments in life

## 9.

Take control of your life
You have the choice to be miserable or to be happy
To be successful or be a failure
And most of all
A choice to be a good and righteous person
Or a person of deceit and evil

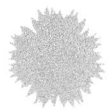

**10.**

Isn't it surprising you think you know a person because
of the years you have known them?
But you are wrong; they are not what you thought they were

## 11.

Why would I want all the wealth in the world?
Why would I want all the fame and glory
Where I don't know who are my real friends and enemies?
Yes, it's true
There are those who have both fame and glory
Yet, they don't have peace within themselves
Out of desperation, their only way is to drown in drugs and alcohol
And then find they are more confused
That will lead them to self-destruction and even death
I don't envy them
As long as I have enough to live, surrounded with people I trust and love
I feel I am the luckiest person on Earth

**12.**

Friends that last forever and loving families
These are priceless, worth more than the riches in the world
They give us the reasons that life is worth living

## 13.

At times to be hurt is needed
To remind us that we are not as invincible as we perceived
we were
Disappointments are at times essential
To awaken us to the realities of life
That not everything is always within our reach
Failures can at times act as a catalyst for us to strive more
And can be a tool to open the door for success

**14.**

Don't fret about your previous mistakes
Be focused on the present
Concentrate on your strongest point
Thus in time, you will reach the pinnacle of success

**15.**

Nothing is permanent: people, places, surroundings change
At times for better or for worse
Though at times we resist changes
It is inevitable; it will happen one day
To avoid frustrations, disappointments and expectations, one must always be flexible and be prepared for when it happens

**16.**

Even though it took us numerous years to realise and open our
eyes to the stupid things we did
Change is always worth it and necessary irrespective of our age
This is in order to make the remaining years of life memorable
and enjoyable

## 17.

Fear of the unknown is one of the reasons we are reluctant to
do the things out of our comfort zone
But once we have decided to take the risk and have
succeeded, the benefits are endless
Then, we will never look back
For those of us who have failed
At least we can learn from our mistakes
Thus inspiring us to do it better next time around

**18.**

We sometimes wish that things would be different from the present
However, just counting our blessings and the things we are enjoying now
Will ease our disappointments and frustrations
Accept that in life
We cannot have everything we wish for

**19.**

Our kids are the reflections of us
If we give them love, support, inspire them to do things they like
For sure they will do the same for their own kids – just a cycle of life.

**20.**

Never cease loving, caring, believing and being positive
These are what life is all about
They are the reasons that make our journey in life easier, meaningful and inspirational

**21.**

We should never pass the day without thanks for our blessings
Each day is a challenge we have to face
Each day is another day on which we will be able to build our dreams and foundations for a better tomorrow
Don't let it be wasted

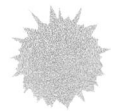

**22.**

Yes, we are humbled by our own experience
A great person will hold his head up high
Regardless of the outcome
And graciously accept the defeat
As long as you do your best, it's all that matters
Of course, people can sometimes be cruel
Criticising and insulting and making fun of you – an ugly side to human behaviour
However after the fall
You must do some soul-searching
And start to question yourself about your priorities in life

**23.**

We should always know our own limitations or know when to stop
At times we are so immersed in our fame, success and glory
That we think we are invincible or indestructible
Soon we realise that we are not

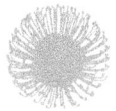

**24.**

Each of us has a cross to carry
Each of us will go through trying times in our lives
But with our faith, our trust in Him
And with the support of families and friends
The crosses will be bearable
To carry throughout our journey in life

## 25.

I could feel the pain of the parents
Worrying about their kids' futures
Despite our very good intentions
To guide our kids, the correct path to follow
We must remember
That the influence of the environment, friends
Is stronger than the love we have for them
Today's culture is so different from when we were young
Nothing much we can do but to let them
Know that we are always there for them
Regardless
Such a tough role to be a parent

## 26.

There are the moments
That are precious
That we tend to relive and remember
Each time, it makes us happy and puts a smile on our faces
But there are memories that should be forgotten and instead serve as a lesson learned in our lives

## 27.

It is in the realm of one's experiences
That we learn to know
What is right or wrong
What is ethical or not
But some are just too stubborn
To accept their past mistakes
Relentlessly doing the same mistakes
Over and over again

**28.**

Regardless of the pain we feel
From the loss of our loved ones
We, the living, should be strong
Continue to move on for the sake
Of the living loved ones
We still have

**29.**

Test of the real character of a person is shown
By how they react or respond
To every unexpected event or situation
That confronts them

**30.**

Giving does not mean expecting
To receive in return
Loving does not mean
Changing the person for your own self intent
Believing does not mean being blinded
And shielded from facing the truth
Hoping does not mean not realising your
Own limitations and inadequacies

**31.**

Love is given freely
The takers should not take it for granted
Instead it should be cherished, nurtured
And protected
Once it disappears, you will be missing
The most important thing in your life

**32.**

At times we are so much concerned
On wanting so many things in our lives
Thus, taking too much clutter within
That we fail to identify and prioritise
The most important thing in our lives

### 33.

When blessings and good fortune
Come in abundance
We tend to take these for granted
But soon realise the loss
Once these are taken away from us

**34.**

We try as much as we can
To hold on to something
No matter how precious it is
There will come a time
To have to let it go and move on

## 35. I BELIEVE

That life does not need to be perfect
Imperfection challenges, motivates,
stimulates
The desire to grow and be a better person
Imperfection makes us humble
Helps us to accept
Things we cannot change
Imperfection enables us to see life
From a different perspective
Perhaps so we can see more in-depth meaning
To what life is all about

## 36.

It's not about making it to the top
Being successful and famous, in your career
It's all about giving back
Generously to the community
Some of your time
Specially to those needing the most

### 37.

Demons, monsters, evil are very true
Yet we cannot see them
Because they are lurking within ourselves
Fight and conquer them we must
For if we fail
Eventually they will poison and overtake
Our body, mind and soul

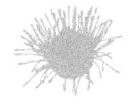

## 38. SUCCESS

A word which equates to hard work, perseverance and determination
Sadly, at times
These are not a guarantee or recipe for success.
Though, however hurtful it may be
We have to accept things as they are Changing your focus and directions will help
Possibly this time the road to success will be on your side

## 39. I BELIEVE

Prayers are not the only way to talk, to communicate with God. There are other ways such as simple acts of kindness to others. I am close with nature while working in the garden. I can show my appreciation of all the beautiful creations He had given us. I am a good mother, grandmother, friend and respect for others.

    I can show Him I am following one of the commandments 'Love thy neighbour' and I strongly believe what matters most is following all that He preaches. These are more potent ways of expressing your love for Him.

**40.**

Who said miracles do not exist anymore?
From the moment I open my eyes each morning
I see the sun shining in the sky
Or hear the sound of the rain
Pouring down on my roof
I see life in it.
Beautiful creations from God
Enjoying the sun
Feasting from the pouring rain, the crops that we planted
bearing its fruit
I see miracles in these
Indeed, about the harmonious relationship of nature and mankind
A simple thing I can say is
'Miracle of life'

**41.**

Loving someone has its negative side
You feel the pain when you see them hurting
You worry and pray that nothing bad will happen to them.
You wish and hope that they will be able to cope with the challenges along the way
However I will say
These are only a small price to pay for the blessings, blissful happiness and joy of having someone to love
And in turn to be loved

## 42. EVERYTHING CHANGES

People, places, things surrounding us
We change through the years
Physically, emotionally, mentally and spiritually
Loving someone means continually
Accepting them, what they are today
Rather than what they were yesterday

**43.**

While 'love, understanding, compassion' are
The foundations of all Goodness in the world
'Hatred, greed, hunger for power' are the very reasons
Evil exists here on earth

**44.**

Being happy doesn't need to be expensive
Happiest I am, in my backyard admiring my flowers, trees, plants
Happiest I am each time I tickle the ivory keys playing my favourite piece
There are wonders in life that make people happy
That money can't buy

**45.**

With my strong faith in 'Him'
Plus the love and support of
My families, friends I know
I can get through all the
Challenges I face
As I walk through the journey of life.

## 46. LETTING IT GO

Does not mean forgetting the past
It is merely a preparation
For the new beginning
New life, new hope
Use your past as an inspiration
For a better future

**47.**

After grieving, the healing process
Is a long road to tackle
With your strong faith in Him
Positive attitude in life
You can do it in time

**48.**

Death will always leave
A gaping hole in our heart
It will take time to heal
But all the beautiful memories
Will always be treasured and kept
In our hearts

## 49.

It is very frustrating
When your best intentions
Are often misunderstood
And misinterpreted in
A negative way
But then again we
Have to realise that
We cannot please everybody, every time

**50.**

I still believe that all of us
Regardless of who and what we are
Still have a soft spot and have
Some kindness in our hearts

**51.**

It is what we reveal of ourselves
That could give others the wrong impression
That makes us vulnerable
To different kinds of deceit
Thus having advantage taken
Of our generosity and good intentions

**52.**

An act of kindness
Done wholeheartedly
Can go a long way
More than you realise
One way we can all
Make a difference

**53.**

Quite a few times
You thought you knew a person well
But really you don't

## 54. I BELIEVE

One of the many ways to achieve peace within
Is not to compare yourself with others
But learn to accept and be
Who you are and the best of
What you are

**55.**

My great admiration is for the people who
In spite of all the adversities, heartaches and
tribulations they have gone through
Manage to stand on their own two feet
Are successful in life
And also help others

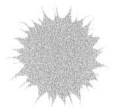

**56.**

Most of us love to dwell on the past
We should let it go and move on
What matters is the present
The past is only memories
That will inspire us not to make
The same mistakes, but strengthen us
To aspire to be better and stronger

**57.**

In our younger days, we were so eager
To learn new things, venture into new experiences
Enjoy each time we went through
Extensive knowledge we so desired
But it is in our mature years we can
Comprehend, understand and appreciate
Appreciate everything we have learned and experienced
through the years

**58.**

As much as we love, cherish
Adore our grandkids
We must keep in mind
That they are not ours
The parents have the last say
In any decision or in any
Other future circumstances

**59.**

What's the best thing about being retired?
First and foremost, there is no pressure of work
You don't have to prove yourself each time
It's a chance to discover oneself and develop new interest in life
You have the time to look after grandkids and the best of all
No Monday blues, every day is a holiday
We worked hard before and
We all deserve a happy and joyous retirement

## 60.

We don't expect to live forever
So make each day a Celebration of Life
Each day thanking Him for
All the graces we do have
Savour each precious moment
You spend with loved ones, families and friends
If you fail to do so
One day you will realise
You missed the most important
Things in your life
That money couldn't buy.

## 61.

Others hide their sorrows through their smiles
Others hide their fears by acting fearlessly
Others hide their insecurity by being boastful all the time
Others hide their inferiority by acting superior to everyone
At times the things that we see are not really what they are
There more depths and meanings to consider before judging others

## 62. I BELIEVE

True friendship does not take a day to make
Just like Rome was not built in a day
It takes fine wine years to age and to attain perfection
Friendship takes years to develop
Those memories good ones and bad ones
You share together
Accepting of one's faults and inadequacies
Understanding and forgiveness
And if the time comes when you won't see each other again
Beautiful memories of friendship
That no one can take away from you
Will remain embedded in your heart

## 63. I BELIEVE

Quality of life and success of a person
Cannot be measured
By being rich
Nor by being famous
It can only be measured
If you have inner peace
A loving family
And real friends who always care for you

**64.**

Children laughing and playing
Hugs and kisses of your grandkids, kids
The beautiful aroma of your wife's cooking
The sight of the magnificent flowers, plants blossoming
Sometimes the best things in life to be enjoyed
Are just
The simplest things in life

**65.**

Waking up each day without expecting anything
Always thanking each day for my blessings enjoyed
Savouring each minute, moment, of what life has to offer
Enjoying to the fullest the beautiful surroundings
The beautiful people such as loved ones and friends
Whom have given me joy and made my journey in life
So interesting and meaningful
And most of all
Had a part of making me what I am today

## 66. SUCCESS IS

How quickly you get up
Each time you fall
And never lose hope

## 67. ON RETIREMENT

I was often asked these questions
Are you bored being retired?
How do you fill up your time?
I just smile
I don't have to explain anything
Because I know within
I am enjoying every minute of being retired
How can you be bored sharing precious moments with
your loved ones?
How can you be bored when you can explore and
re-invent yourself?
How can you be bored when now you can do things you are passionate about?
How can you be bored if you keep challenging yourself and stimulating your brain
At times I wish there were twenty-eight hours in a day
To fill up my very busy life

## 68. CALAMITY

How easy it is to unmake years of hard work, sacrifices, time and effort
To watch them disappear in seconds
These are the feelings of the people affected by disasters and calamities
Really a tough word we live in
The very reason why we should acknowledge each day as a blessing
Each day as a challenge

# My Wisdoms

**1.**

Live in this world not as people expect you to be but as you really want to be.
One element towards achieving happiness in life

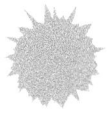

**2.**

Never fear to take risks and be out of your comfort zone
It is the only way to find your ultimate strength and capabilities
That at times you are not even aware of

**3.**

It takes courage to forgive
But it takes twice the courage to ask for forgiveness

**4.**

Expect the unexpected
Expect the inevitable
Change the things within your grip, but don't despair For the things you can't change – that's how life is

**5.**

Evil disguises itself in many forms
It is up to us to {whether we } fall to {into} its treacherous trap

**6.**

Intricate and complexity of human emotions and minds are difficult to comprehend
At times you think you know a person well
But soon realise you don't

**7.**

One of the reasons why some people are miserable and discontented in their lives
Is because they are always comparing themselves with others
Instead of just being themselves

**8.**

With so many things kept cluttered in our hearts
We fail to find a space for Him to reside in our hearts
The sign of modern times

**9.**

Don't waste your time regretting your past mistakes
Or you will live forever miserably
You are then unable to look forward to brighter days in your life

## 10.

The only way to be non-judgemental is to accept people
for what they are
Be it a difference of religion, culture belief or value
Each one of us can start by
Thus making this world an ideal place to live

**11.**

There are times when what you perceive about yourself
Is not necessarily the same
As what others think of you

**12.**

It does not matter how old you are, provided you know
your own limitations
You can still follow your dream and work for it
You will be surprised by what you can achieve

**13.**

One of the many things I have learned from life
It is far better to not expect anything and be surprised
Than to be bitterly disappointed over something you were expecting to happen

**14.**

Words are so powerful
They are like a sword
They can pierce you right through your heart

**15.**

It's not about what you have and
It's not about when you made it to the top
It's all about being passionate and happy with what you do
It's also all about being at peace with yourself, others and God

**16.**

Quite often many words are left unspoken,
Either too hurtful or too intense
These words would not be enough to express it

**17.**

At times we get hurt by the very people we trusted
But then again, being unable to trust anyone can make our lives miserable

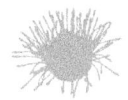

**18.**

A person who pretends too much will at the end be confused about the difference between reality and fantasy

**19.**

Always be what you are and let people
Accept you for who you are and not what they think you are

**20.**

One day you will realise the things you take for granted are as precious as gold

**21.**

You learn hundred times more from life's experiences than you learn in the classroom

**22.**

Being a parent you learn to love unconditionally
By making self-sacrifices as a parent you become more sensitive to all the issues around
Wishing one day your kids will learn how to tackle and survive in this tough world

## 23.

Just live for today
What is important is the present
Yesterday is just a memory, where the good is to be treasured
and the bad should be forgotten
Make another day of hope and blissful living

## 24.

When we stop doing the things we are passionate about
That's the time we stop living

**25.**

We criticise others
Based on what we perceive
To be right or wrong

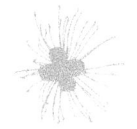

**26.**

When the tears dry up and stop flowing
That's the time you can
Feel the intensity of your pain

**27.**

You have done your best
And your best is still not good enough
Don't despair
It's probably not meant to happen
Luck and destiny are in full control

## 28.

Believing and dreaming is one thing
Taking actions on what you believe is another thing
Just believing and having the passion are the best weapons for success

**29.**

Experiences in life
Enrich one's knowledge
Always the best mentors
In your life

**30.**

When one becomes overwhelmed and cannot speak
It's best to keep silent
Then the silence becomes more powerful than words

**31.**

Living in the past will only cause
Heartaches and frustrations
Deter us from moving forward

**32.**

It's love that makes us do the impossible
Can't be seen, but can be felt
It's so powerful
It can turn a person into a beast
Or a beast into an angel

**33.**

It's not about life
It's all about
How you live your life

**34.**

Fear not Death
It's only the beginning
Of a new life

**35.**

Truth hurts
But no matter how hurtful it is
It is an effective way
To bring a change

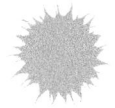

**36.**

Music can connect people
Can bring them together
Regardless of religion, gender and belief

**37.**

It is what we make our life
That makes life itself
Full of challenges and surprises

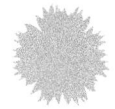

**38.**

It's easier to love than to hate
But some people do it
The other way around

**39.**

Hope always bring comfort
Strength to each endeavour

**40.**

Greed, hungry for power are akin to drugs
So addictive once tasted
You don't know how
And when to stop

**41.**

Some people would quit
Without even trying
One way of missing out

**42.**

At times in some circumstances
You have to please first yourself before others

**43.**

Such a beautiful gesture of friendship
They are always there to help you
In time of your needs
Support you when needed
Guide and lead you

**44.**

Challenging yourself
Insatiable quest
For perfection and knowledge
These are effective tools
To be successful in life

## 45.

At times we need a big fall and disappointment
To awaken us to our senses
To know that we are not invulnerable
As we thought we were
Restores the goodness within which we once had.

**46.**

At times we are more concerned
With what others would say or think
Thus affecting our judgement
To act in the right and sensible way

## 47.

A life fully treasured
Fully enjoyed
Is worth all the richness
In the world
Priceless

## 48.

At times you will be surprised
That a stranger you met before
Can one day help you
In time of need

## 49.

Yesterday's lessons and
Soul-searching experiences
Are needed to make the
Present foundation effective
And stronger for a better
And successful tomorrow

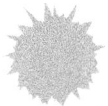

**50.**

It is what you believe
Convictions, principles in life
That will lead you
to what you are today

**51.**

We sometimes falter and fail
But what matters most
Is how quickly we stand up
And have the courage to
Do it all over again
Till we have succeeded and attained
What we were aiming for

**52.**

There are things in life
That we perceive
Are not what they really are
And sometimes even the smartest person
Can be deceiving, often times
Evil can hide and pose in the shadow of goodness

**53.**

Old friends are worth keeping
But there will also be a room for new ones
You never know
You can still find new ones worth keeping

**54.**

It's not about the quantity or length of time you spent on earth
It's all about the quality of life you make for yourself and others

**55.**

At times the things that
We see are only illusions
You have to dig deeper
Analyse, understand
What really lies beneath the surface

**56.**

I want to be accepted as I am
Not how others want me to be

**57.**

When in doubt and confused
Listen to your heart
It will take you there {to where you should be}

**58.**

Don't let frustrations, disappointments overtake you
Instead, make them your friends
Strive more and aim higher
Till the pinnacle of success is achieved

**59.**

Dreams are only the start
Taking action is the ultimate beginning
To make your dreams come true

## 60.

There's nothing more glorious
Than to hear and see
The laughter and sound
Of happy kids
Playing in my house

**61.**

Each day you wake up
Is already a blessing
Regardless of what you do
Make each day as special as can be

**62.**

Denial is the deadliest hindrance
To making a change and moving forward

### 63.

You cannot achieve
Inner peace
Unless
Envy and hatred
No longer
Reign in your heart

**64.**

You cannot run forever
For all your problems and fear
Will catch you unexpectedly one day
With dire consequences

**65.**

It's not about the quantity of time
That you spend with your loved ones
It's all about the quality
How you spend the time with them
That's what matters most

**66.**

Hope is the only thing we try to hold on
Amidst our frustrations
Disappointments and sorrows
Without it we could not move on
And have the courage to face what lies ahead

### 67.

Grandkids
What priceless gifts
Given to us by our own kids
Won't trade them for anything in the world

## 68.

Lots of things in our lives are so simple
We make it so complicated
Hence at the end we are trapped
With our own wrongdoing

## 69.

A beautiful smile can melt anyone's heart
Especially the smiles from your loved ones

# Reflective Contemplations

## A Tribute to Life

# Lorna Ramirez

Published in Australia by Lorna Ramirez

First published in Australia February 2018

This edition published 2018

Copyright © Lorna Ramirez 2018

Cover design, typesetting: Chameleon Print Design

The right of Lorna Ramirez to be identified as the Author of the Work has been asserted in accordance with the Copyright, Designs and Patents Act 1988.

All rights reserved. No part of this publication may be reproduced, stored in a retrieval system, or transmitted, in any form or by any means without the prior written permission of the publisher, nor be otherwise circulated in any form of binding or cover other than that in which it is published and without a similar condition being imposed on the subsequent purchaser.

Ramirez, Lorna

*Reflective Contemplations: A Tribute to Life*

ISBN: 978-0-6482130-2-4

pp126

# Acknowledgements

***Special Thanks to Alyssa Cary
my Personal Assistant***

**Dedicated To**

*My loving husband, Claro*
*Grandchildren Alyssa and Amelia*
*Children and their partners:*
*Carlo and Marie*
*Maria and Steve*
*My sister Victoria Polon*

# Preface

This book is a collection of articles I had written and were published at *The Philippine Times* Melbourne newspaper. The book also included my original written poems, inspirational messages and quotes. Any similarities to other writings are purely coincidental.

My love and close bonding with my families, loved ones and friends and my strong connection with GOD had inspired me to write all the beautiful passages and inspirational messages'

I believe as we mature our perspective and priorities in life will change, hence I am happy to share to all people; my life experiences, knowledge gained, lessons learned, my convictions and the philosophies I had developed throughout my life

I hope that the readers will enjoy as well as relate to the topics and sensitive issues that were presented in this book *Reflective Contemplations*.

—**By Lorna Ramirez**

# A.
# Contemplations

# 1
## A Tribute To Life

Waking up each day is a celebration of life. A life of new beginning. To be able to cherish once again, and enjoy life itself. It becomes routine and normal for all of us to wake up each day and we have taken it for granted. Then one day we learn that there are those who are not given a chance to do it all again. Instead they have succumbed to deep slumber, the pangs of death came and the bereft of life has been taken away from them. Leaving loved ones, families and friends in pain and sorrows. Let's appreciate each day, waking up thankful that we are still here, enjoying the breath of life… Let's pray for those who were not given a chance to do so.

I vividly remember, during my university years I had a close friend. She was pretty, smart, and belonged to a wealthy family. She was very popular in our engineering campus, and being an only child she had everything in life. On our final exam there was shocking news, she had died in her sleep. We were all devastated.

This experience made me see life from a different perspective. Treasuring and enjoying each moment shared with families and friends. Before and after waking up acknowledging and thanking God for all the blessings received for the day. I always say "I love you" to my loved ones, because I do not know if there will be a chance for me to say it tomorrow. Each day I try to do things that I am passionate about such as tickling the ivory keys, writing, gardening, and appreciating everything that I have. At times we should try to help others, especially those who need it the most. But there will be instances where you will get frustrated and upset when you are generous and people will try to take advantage of you, one ugly side of human nature. Indeed we do all have our weaknesses and imperfections. However being aware of it and trying to overcome it is much better than doing nothing at all.

As the popular saying goes, "life is too short to be miserable," so let's live life to the fullest. Don't let envy, greed, and jealousy reign to our hearts, and in failing to do so you will not find inner peace within yourself and your fellowmen.

An excerpt from my book,
*My Innermost Thoughts*

---

We should never pass the day
Without giving thanks
For our blessings,
Each day is a challenge we have to face
Each day is another day on which
We will be able to build
Our dreams and foundations
For a better tomorrow.

Don't let it be wasted.

# 2
# A Tribute to all Mothers

To be a mother is the noblest job of all, but the most underrated. It is the very reason why it should always be celebrated each year. It is an acknowledgment of all the hard work, sacrifices, juggling the time for those who are working, just to have and share quality and precious time with their family.

Being a mother myself, I still worry for my children no matter how old they are. Now that they have children of their own, my role as a mother never ends. The work continues, giving the love and care to the grandchildren.

A mother's heart is so strong, it can withstand the pain inflicted by loved ones, or even by their own children. A mother's love is a selfless love that keeps on forgiving and giving, until there is no more left for them to give.

A mother's love is so understanding and supportive, guiding their children in every possible way. However at times, children can go astray, the influence of friends and environments can be stronger than the care and love we give them. I feel the pain of the parents going through this.

Indeed, mother's love is lasting, endless, unconditional, and beyond comprehension. No one can fathom what a mother's love is, unless you are a mother.

Excerpt from
*My Passion My Calling*:

It is the mother's heart
That children can find
Assurance of being loved
It is in the mother's arms
That children can find solace
And comfort, but
It is in the mother's hugs and kisses
That they can find the real joy
Of being loved and most of all
Being special and cared for

# 3
## Father's of Today

Arguably fathers are the wind beneath the wings of family units and of institutions; a protector, defender, bread winner, and the guiding light. Yes, things have changed. It is the evolution of the new fathers of today in contrast to the far cry from the old years where household work and looking after children was solely the responsibilities of mothers.

I grew up in a family with my father as the bread winner and my mother who stayed at home to care for us. However, my parents broke the hold of gender roles and encouraged us to pursue university degrees in order to have a better and more successful future.

With more and more women in the workforce pursuing their careers and ambitions, there is no alternative but for a husband to actively do a fair share of household work, especially in countries like Australia where domestic help is uncommon and child care services are too expensive.

Because of the present insecurities of today such as redundancies, layoffs, factory closures, and dependence on the incomes of mothers, some fathers decide to be stay at home dads which was an unthinkable situation in my time. Whatever happened to the "Male ego"? I believe that couples at present are being practical and sensible in their endeavours that are unsolicited by forced gender roles. And why not?

The family and looking after the children are the most important thing in the world.

With the advocacy of equal rights, we are seeing more and more husbands looking after the children and the home. When I was baby-sitting my grandchildren and attending a mother's group, some who were actively involved were fathers and their children; a beautiful scene to watch and witness. Hence the evolution of what fathers of today are.

In this modern era some families consist of two fathers or two mothers and society accepts this as a normal way of life.

Being a father is not an easy job. Fathers have tried to be strong, but deep within they do have a soft spot for their children. In some difficult and crucial situations fathers remain calm and strong, as their children continue to look up to and idolise them.

No matter what the situations in today's technological world, a father's heart and soul never changes. He loves his family to a point that he will protect them to his last breath of life.

Fathers are disciplinarians, yet they are caring, affectionate and loving. In turn children will look for partners who resemble their parents, and will take after the characteristics of their parents, their role models form childhood. Fathers especially have a great influence and important role in their families.

We should give credit and acknowledgement to single fathers who act the roles of both parents. The sacrifices that he will do to be able to achieve a healthy and happy life for his children and beyond compare.

Suffice to say that it is paramount and relevant to celebrate father's day, not only during this month of September but all year round to give fathers the recognition of the sacrifices and their active involvement in moulding their children to be the best of what they can be.

Needless to say, fathers make the life in family institution rewarding and worth living.

Excerpt from my book
*My Passion My Calling*

'To a husband'
Through the years pass
The stronger bond still exists
Both of us had changed physically
But we have grown stronger together
With a more mature outlook in life
Thus the love for one another
Continues to flow
Regardless of all obstacles
We have endured
As we walk through our journry
Of our lives
Proud to have him as my husband
My soulmate and my real
Best Friend

# 4
# Acceptance Versus Tolerance

Acceptance and tolerance are two words that majority of people do not know the difference. The truth is they are world apart. Acceptance is the higher level of tolerance. Tolerance means you can tolerate something but not necessarily accepting it.

In the modern era, most of us will show tolerance to sensitive issues such as race, religion and most especially to the LGBT ( Lesbian, Gay, Bisexual and Transgendered ), but are they widely accepted by the majority of the population?

At the early century in medieval Europe, homosexuality was considered a sodomy even punishable by death. Even today they were called names such as queer, gay, faggot etc. At times families disown their own offspring because of this issue.

In 1980's the gay community had a setback. They were antagonised because of the Aid's epidemic. A big blow to them. Through the years with more and more celebrities and entertainers coming out of their closets plus the role of the media had helped significantly the war against homophobic.

Indeed Homosexual (LGBT) had gone a long way since the early centuries and even in the early 20$^{th}$ century. Is it because we are more educated now and the influence of social media changed the way people think or are we just became more rational, open minded and people nowadays are not conservative and religious than before?

that we are all different and loving someone with the same gender does not mean their love is inferior than those who love the opposite sex. I do believe that a person will be the one to decide who they really are and not to be dictated and pressured by the society. Their mind, heart and soul will decide what gender they are comfortable with. Regardless of what they chose (choose) they deserve to be happy.

What will be your reaction if one of your children will inform you that they are different? It will be frustrating of course, but there is nothing much we can do, we should support them. Its not their fault it is just unfortunate they were born in a wrong body.

It is quite timely that this issue is in my latest book, Moments of Love, Lust and Ecstasy. I never expected it to be an issue this year in Australia.

Very interesting to see the result of the poll about the same sex marriage. Whatever the result will be, we should respect the decision of the majority. If it is a yes vote perhaps its time for us to reflect and embrace the word acceptance, anyway that is what the world needs now!

Excerpts from my book
*My Innermost Thoughts*

Acceptance

Its easy to love the lovable

Its easy to accept people

Who share our beliefs and convictions

Its easy to love families and friends

It will take courage for us

To love and accept people

Who are different unlovable

This would be a peaceful place

If we tried to accept and respect everyone

Regardless of gender race or religion

And other differences

# 5
## Fear of the Unknown

Excerpt from my Book
*My Innermost Thoughts*

Fear of the unknown is one
Of the reasons we are reluctant
To do things out of our comfort zone
But once we decided to take risk
And have succeeded
The benefits are endless
Then we will never look back
However for those who have failed
At least we can learn from our mistakes
Thus inspiring us to do better next time around

In today's environment, we are witnessing terrorism attacks in public places, concerts, the random unreasonable shootings in public places, schools, our fear of the unknown is at the highest level. Its so sad if we succumb to this. We will become prisoners of ourselves and the fear will deter us from enjoying our lives.

Fear of the unknown is akin to the fear of doing things out of our comfort zone. The fear of failure is always in our mind. Successful people take risk, but with calculated risk. They do have alternative plan if things did not work out. They managed to assess and learn from their mistakes that gave them motivation to do it all over again till they succeeded.

Lack of knowledge is also a contributing factor for our fear of the unknown and most often the fear is unsubstantiated hence preventing them to experiment, take risk and progress will never be achieved.

Childhood tragedy, traumatic experiences and unhappy childhood are also amongst the reasons for our fear of the unknown. They would prefer to be on the safe side, scared of changes, and prefer a stable and constant surroundings.

Fear of the unknown will deter us to tap our outmost potential. We won't be able to explore our hidden talents. We should always remember that life itself is a gamble and venturing into different avenues in life are at times worth fulfilling and satisfying and definitely one of the recipes for success.

Indeed, there are ways to overcome your fear. First and foremost is to analyse and comprehend your fear. Do research and gather facts. The worst thing is doing nothing and not knowing if it is worth a try, thus missing opportunities and the failure of the realisation of your dreams to come true. Another one is by doing it slowly facing your fear one step at a time till you conquer your fear. You can also read inspiring books, talk to people, ask for the support of your families and friends.

Year 1977 when we decided to migrate to Australia. We had our doubts. Both of us had a good paying job, financially stable, but we chose to migrate. Going to a country with no families and friends and with young children was a gamble. We had overcome our fear and we never looked back. The best decision we had.

Regardless of how old you are, you can still face your fear. Learn new things, be adventurous after all, life is too short to be doing nothing!

# 6
## *Dad...The Hero*

Most of us are fascinated with *super heroes*. Children always have their favourite super hero but their real living super heroes through their eyes are their Dads.

The sons perceive their father as an idol, wishing to be like him when they grow up. The daughters when they were young view their fathers as their knights in shining armours ready to help and protect them from everything.

Not all fathers are worthy being good fathers, but generally fathers always love, care and are the ultimate protectors of the families, hence they are the strength of a family institution.

Dads are always fun to be with. They play soccer, football and other sports with their children. A father will be there for his family, he is expected to be responsible and carry the weight on all the problems of the family and of course with the help of his wife.

The interactions of the children with fathers during early childhood will develop the children personalities in their adulthood. His involvement within the family is critical and important to a successful family ties and family bonding.

Nowadays, more and more of mothers are in the workforce, thus the role of a fathers in the $21^{st}$ century are demanding as ever. Dads taking huge responsibilities in household works, looking after the children and at times they can do it even better than their wives.

Fathers are expected to be the disciplinarians, but with kindness and softness in their hearts. Quite difficult to be achieved, however as always they can managed it efficiently and effectively.

All children when they were young enjoyed to be sitting on their father's shoulder. They felt tall and loved to see everything around them. This is what fathers do.

Father's love is unconditional. They will always be there for their children, but they do not condone wrong behaviour and attitude. They are firm in their decisions, yet always open to suggestions and ideas. They are willing to accept mistakes, these are the qualities of an ideal and a good father to his children

Father of a Bride, a movie made in 1991, typifies how a father can be overprotective to his daughter. The movie also exemplified how a father feels when his daughter decided to get married and start her own family. A comedy movie but I am sure fathers can relate to this.

An excerpt from my 2<sup>nd</sup> book

*My Passion, My Calling*

---

Through the eyes of the children
Their parents are their role models and heroes
Therefore it is the responsibility
Of every parent to set high standard
To be able to produce
Future responsible adults

# 7
## Love and Acceptance

Of human and divine love; which love is the greatest of them all, will you be able to sacrifice one for the other? Indeed a very sensitive and controversial topic. The answers will depend on your own perspective in life.

Whatever you choose, both of them have one thing in common – acceptance. Acceptance of responsibilities, commitments and sacrifices for the one you love.

*The Cardinal*, film of 1963 exemplified what divine love is. A young priest had to choose between the life of his sister and her unborn child. The head of the baby had to be crushed to save the mother, yet being a priest he did not allow this to happen, resulting in the death of the mother. That made him question his faith.

He requested a two year sabbatical leave and went to Vienna Austria to teach. There he met and fell in love with a girl, however the priest did not violate his vows of chastity and in the end he had chosen divine love. His love for God was stronger in his heart than human love.

Same heartaches and sorrow will be felt by a mother, who has no choice but to give up her newborn child for adoption for the sake of its welfare and future. Sacrifices have to be made for the sake of your loved ones.

Loving someone is not easy. You have to accept the whole package, his or her own imperfections.

Loving does not mean changing the person for your own personal intent. You will always feel pain and hurt whenever you see your loved one suffer. You will always worry about them.

But then again it's only a small price to pay for the joy and happiness that you feel, of loving and being loved.

Here is my unpublished poetry about love:

Love encompasses everything
Does not know boundaries
It is so strong
It will conquer all
Along its path
Does not care who you are
Regardless of gender, status,
Or beliefs.
Makes a strong man cry
And a weak man strong

# 8
# Realities of Life

Just a simple, gentle squeeze on your hand from someone you love, can mean a thousand things. A wonderful token of love, affection, care, understanding, support and much more. It can be easily felt within your heart, a simple gesture, yet stronger and powerful, than any spoken words.

I do believe, it's not only saying "I love you," but it's all about caring and even doing sacrifices if needed for someone you love.

Love for me is the essence of what life is all about, happy are those who are surrounded with loved ones; faithful friends, and most of all loving families. These are the very people who will always be there for you regardless of what you are.

Of course it is not always easy for us to make choices, at times we falter along the way. People will despise, criticise, but you can still manage to be strong. You know there are those who believe in you. They are the reason for your inspiration to fight back until you can achieve your dreams and goals in life.

However there are those who are consumed by success, forgetting where they started. When everything had been taken away from them, they realised who their real friends are. They sought out the loving arms of their families.

We don't have to please everyone, there are people who won't appreciate you no matter what you do. Instead, concentrate more on those who love and care for you. They will always be there for you, thus making your journey easier and more meaningful.

You can read more of my inspirational messages from my two books. *My Innermost Thoughts* is a compilation of my poems, wisdoms, and beliefs. *My Passion My Calling* is a memoir, encompassing my journey as an author.

An excerpt from *My Innermost Thoughts*: "Why would I want all the wealth in the world? Why would I want all the fame and glory, where I don't know who are my real friends and enemies? Yes it's true, there are those who have both fame and glory, yet they don't have the peace within themselves. Out of desperation, their only way is to drown in drugs and alcohol, and then find themselves more confused, that will lead them to self-destruction and even death. I don't envy them. I think as long as I have enough to live, surrounded with people I love and trust. *I feel I am the luckiest person on earth.*"

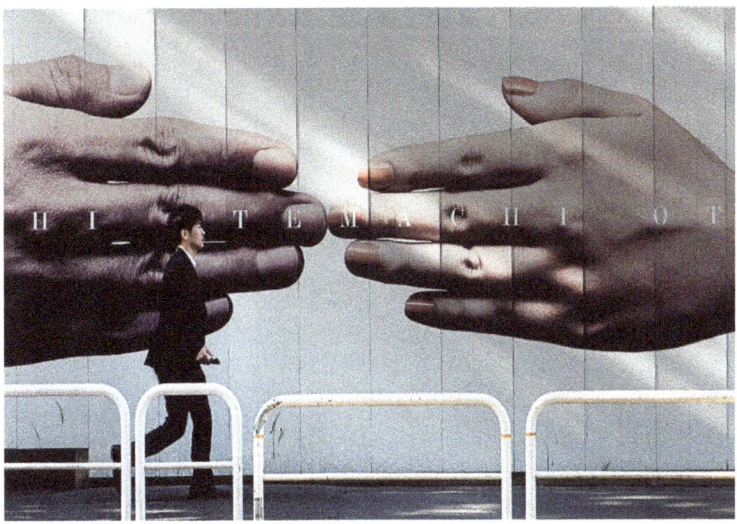

## 9
## What's in a Smile

A beautiful smile can melt anyone's heart, but what is really in a smile that inspires a poet to write, a musician to write songs about it, and Leonardo da Vinci to paint the Mona Lisa; the lady with a mysterious smile that captivates and fascinates all of us? Indeed do not underestimate the power of a smile.

How often do we meet and encounter strangers on the streets, shopping malls and indifferent places? Just a swift fleeting glance from them followed by a smile can mean a lot of things such as greetings; hello, how are you, wishing you the best of the day. A gesture that is more potent and powerful way of communicating other than words. The moment when you see loved ones, friends and relations, before uttering a word a smile from their faces say it all.

A smile is a symbol and image of our emotions and an expression of our inner self but nonetheless not all smiles are genuine and sincere. There are smiles that are deceiving, hurtful and insulting which is an ugly side of the human nature. There are those people who however, smile while hiding their frustration, sorrow and grief. They are the courageous ones who remain positive and continue to move on.

We always smile in front of the camera because we want to be remembered as happy contented people who enjoy that very moment when the photo is taken. Who can forget that beautiful smile from your first crush, your first love? A thrilling and exhilarating special moment that we had. Likewise, those gorgeous smiles from your children and your grandchildren will always be cherished in your heart.

When your children and grandchildren were small and were being naughty, a smile from their faces would stop me from being mad. But of course it would not deter me to explain to them the consequences of their actions. Every time we came home from a hard day's work at the office, a smile from the faces of our loved ones would always bring sunshine, joy and relief.

A smile can be infectious. If you are surrounded by people who are happy and smile, you feel comfortable and at ease, and at times you can alleviate your problems. Smiling can also have a tremendous effect on your health by lowering your stress level, hence leaving less negativity and a more positive outlook on life.

This is one of the best quotes from Mother Theresa, a recently canonised saint: "Every time you smile at someone, it is an action of love, a gift to that person, a beautiful thing." An awe inspiring and impressive quote that is always worth remembering.

You can do no wrong by smiling. It is good for the body and smiling symbolises contentment, peace and positive attitude. There is so much anger, negativity and chaos at present, and what the world needs now is smiling and happy people regardless of what the situation is. So keep on smiling and as the popular saying goes: "Smile and the world smiles at you, cry and you will cry alone."

Some original and unpublished quotes about smiles:

A smile can do wonder
It denotes friendship,
Peace and love
A beautiful smile coming from your loved one
Always brings inspiration and love
Especially when you are at the lowest ebb of your life
Just a simple smile
A warm hello
And a gracious thank you
Would make anyone's day
Very special

# 10
# *Spiritual Upliftment*

Excerpt from
*My Innermost Thoughts*

If the food we take nourishes our body
Prayers, meditations and contemplation are the tools
For enriching and uplifting our spiritual souls
Through these we grow to control
Our minds and emotions
Thus bringing to the next level
Where inner peace and satisfaction can be achieved

We spend so much time, effort and money improving our bodies and physical appearances. Companies spent billions of dollars promoting products that claim eternal youth and beauty, but do we take time and effort to improve and nourish our souls? Do you see ads in the media or newspapers promoting the cleansing and purifying of our souls? I don't think so! It doesn't take too much of our time to say prayers, meditate, search for our souls, and yet we hardly do it. Why? Because we are more preoccupied with other worldly things and values such as the quest for glory fame and success. The desire to be the best in whatever we do, the desire to look attractive, punishing ourselves by doing extensive exercise to be fit and perfect. Unfortunately I myself was a victim of these obsessions, but when I had gone through a critical point in my life it made me realise that everything was worthless. Everything that I had aspired for was no longer relevant, and what was more important was the purity of my soul, inner peace, and a strong connection with God.

Sometimes we do need to pause and question ourselves, ask "Is it all worth it?" All the hassles, pressure from work, keeping up with the modern trend, to be the best at what we do; denying ourselves of a much needed break and the special moments that are to be shared with our families and friends.

Saddened that there were people even in the last moments of their lives showed bitterness and discontent to everything around them and never found peace within. Nowadays most of us are more conscience of our image and our status in the community than being aware and mindful of our spiritual needs. Indeed, a sign of modern era.

By migrating to Australia we all have the same goal; to build a new life. There were some who had taken it to the extreme by working seven days a week or doing two jobs at a time. When their health was affected they wished they had spent and taken more of their precious time with their families. It was too late for them but luckily for others it was only a wakeup call.

Even with our children we pressure them to do well at school with our unrealistic expectation which drives them to be depressed and one of the many reasons for youth suicides. As parents we should be perceptive of our children's spiritual and moral developments, in the same way that we do for their academic performance. I believe there should be a balance to be able to produce happy, caring, more responsible adults once they have grown up.

Lastly something to reflect on; *we always mourn for the loss of loved ones and friends, but do we mourn for the loss of one's soul?*

# 11
# The Art of Friendship

LOVE comes in many different forms, and one of them is in the form of *friendship*. A friend can be a mother, sister, or husband, but what I will be discussing in this article is the strong attraction within the interpersonal relationship between two people.

Since time immemorial, all of us have sought and pursued someone to trust, hence friendships blossom. Some friendships continue to exist from childhood up to the present that last forever; truly the best friendships to be desired.

There are times that we can only confide our darkest and innermost secret thoughts to our best friends, and not to our parents or loved ones. This is a token of reliance and loyalty that you are confident to share to your best friend. Friendship is unconditional, forgiving, and has a mutual understanding of each other. However, I strongly believe that in order for friendship to flourish and survive both should take responsibility to nurture it. To make an effort to negotiate what is fair for the interest of both sides.

Oftentimes we develop friendship with a person whom we share the same interests and beliefs. Different personalities can clash, but in rare cases friendships can also develop for two people who have different backgrounds and cultures. Likewise it can also be built based off compatibility either emotionally, spiritually, and psychologically.

A true friend will be able to tell you the truth - even if it hurts – with the intention to do what is best for you. A friend will always be there for you, especially during vulnerable moments in your life. Indeed it is a beautiful expression of friendship.

There are different levels of friendship, the first being your very best friend, and second, casual friends – the friends you associate with time to time and still consider to be a good friend. The third is a group of social friends who are bound together with the same objectives or goals, for example the friends that you have in different organisations doing the same activities or hobbies. The fourth kind are the internet friends such as Facebook friends, a sign of the modern technology of today.

Oftentimes I met with a group of friends who I have lunch with on a weekly basis. When we catch up with each other we share stories of whatever interests us. These are the friends that I have known for the decades since I came to Australia. With them is a day of laughter and jubilation.

One of the best examples of the true definition of what friendship is portrayed in the movie *Beaches*. Presumably most of us have seen this captivating story about two friends. Though they did have differences, her friend stood beside her and helped her go through her difficult times.

So what makes a best friend so special? Is it because you have the privilege of choosing a friend? Or is it because you know that your friend will always be there for you regardless. Whatever the reasons are, one thing is certain: friends will make us feel comfortable and important. They can bring out the best in us, and for me that is what friendships are all about.

An excerpt from
*My Innermost Thoughts*

Friendship
True friendship does not take
A day to make
It takes fine wine years to age
And to attain perfection
Friendship takes years to develop
Those memories good ones and bad ones
You share together
Accepting of ones faults
And indifferences
Understanding and forgiveness
And if time comes when you
Won't see each other again
Beautiful memories of friendship
That no one can take away from you
Will remain embedded
In your heart

# 12
# The Many Faces of Happiness

*An original unpublished poem*

Happy are those who can forgive
Because they will find peace
Within themselves and others
Happy are those who stay connected with God
Because it is the only way to eternal salvation
Happy are those who are willing to share and help others
Because they make a difference in this troubled world we live in
And lastly happy are those who can love and accept people
Because they will be loved in return

Happiness will truly define who, what we are and what our priorities are in life. We go through different stages of happiness as we walk the journey of life. A small child will find happiness by playing with pots and pans or even by pulling tissues from a tissue box, ignoring expensive toys given by dotting parents. Expression of delight and joy on children's' faces when surrounded with candies, chocolates, cakes, and ice cream; those are simple gestures of happiness through the eyes of children.

As we grow older happiness becomes complicated. We set goals, achievements, and power. An ultimate happiness by many of us. For some people, there are those whose happiness can be achieved by sharing and helping others such as missionaries, community workers, soldiers, to name a few. They are special people who have talents that an "Almighty God" has provided them to share.

At the middle of our journey in life a different level of happiness is felt when we meet our soulmate or the love of our life, then becoming a parent. Sheer joy of happiness is experienced when we had our first born child. Our children are an extended version of ourselves, nurture them with love and they will do the same once they have families of their own. No greater happiness can be felt by parents knowing that their children lead a happy and successful life.

My own experience of happiness was that moment where I had the chance to hold my first born granddaughter. From the very first time that I laid eyes on her, I knew that I was blessed to be her grandmother. As I walk through life nearing the end of my journey, my happiness consists of looking after my grandchildren, being there for their first smile, first uttered words, and their first steps. It is an exuberant experience to be a grandmother, and I believe that all grandparents can relate to this.

As a guest speaker at one of the events that I attended I could feel the frustration and loneliness of the elderly. They felt left out and seeking for the attention, love, and care of their families. Fortunately in Australia, we have elderly organisations that are doing a fantastic job to help and entertain them with various activities that can alleviate their loneliness.

At the end we must remember that we will all grow old, and

when the time comes it's up to us to make our own lives interesting regardless of your age.

Akin to the happiness of a child, as we walk through the final journey our happiness becomes simple and uncomplicated. Indeed this is the cycle of life. As we grow older we also realise that *the simplest things in life are often the best.*

# 13
# The Seasons of Life

There is something in the spring season that makes us sprightly and happy. Is it because of the anticipation of warmer days ahead, after the dreary cold winter? For me this is the reason why Spring is my favourite season of the year.

Spring symbolises new hope, new beginning, and new life. For an avid gardener who had done a lot of work fertilising, pruning, re-planting during Winter, this is the time for them to see the fruit of their labour. A bountiful leaves and flowers for the plants, the abundant product of the fruit bearing trees.

Through the window glass in my room I can see at my backyard, my Cherry, Plum, Apple, Peach, and Apricot trees, all showcasing their beautiful blossoms of white, pink, red colours. These blossoms will be turning into fruits at summertime for us to enjoy thus giving nourishment to our bodies.

The season of the year can be compared to our cycles of life. A new born baby resembles spring, symbolises new life, new hope, and will eventually reach its potential at its maturity. Same as the summer season where all plants, shrubs and roses will be at their peak of blooms displaying dazzling array of colours and flowers in all shapes and sizes.

Towards the Autumn season, leaves, flowers beginning to fall, ready for hibernation. For us this is the time for reassessing and reflecting things we had done. By the time Winter comes, some plants and trees will be dormant and for us we will be reaching the end of our journey. Then the whole cycle will start all over again.

Sometimes unexpected event or trauma will happen at any one stage of our lives. A friend of mine lost everything, the house, material possessions, irreplaceable memorabilia in a fire. Synonymous to Winter that is depressing, they managed to pull through. Their strong belief in "GOD" and the help of all their friends and religious congregation, alleviated their sorrows. They stay positive and instead count their blessings that no one lost their lives.

I am now in my twilight years, the Autumn season, slowly reaching the end of the journey. Looking back I am proud of what I had achieved; wonderful, law abiding successful children, well-mannered grandchildren, I am still interacting, connecting and sharing my thoughts and ideas through my writings to all people from all walks of life. If lucky hopefully I will have many more years of Winter seasons to enjoy.

## My Unpublished Poem

Season Of Life
In every stage of life we had
In every Journey of life we tread
In every hardship and Pain
There will always be an end
Just like the winter cold and woeful
Spring will always follow alive and blissful

Forgetting the dark miserable wintery nights

# 14
## Tis' the Season to be Jolly

*(3rd prize, Christmas Writing Competition by the Society Women Writers Victoria)*

'Tis the season to be jolly fa-la-la-la…is the opening song from one of our favourite Christmas songs "Dec The Halls". This is a song filled with joyous moments and a picture perfect atmosphere of Christmas Season. For most of us this is true, especially through the eyes of children, anticipating opening lots of Christmas gifts. For adults, it is the season for endless parties, food gorging and alcohol consumption. For the privileged few, this is the time for luxurious holidays and cruises to exotic places. The Christmas time is also busy for religious group in the preparation in the commemoration of the birth of Christ.

To some people, Christmas do not have any significant importance, examples are; the sick, those without families and friends, people who are sufferings with mental problems or illnesses and the homeless.

For others, Christmas is a time of sorrow. Families who can not afford to give present to loved ones due to financial difficulty. For OFW (Overseas Filipino Workers), an agonising time for them celebrating Christmas away from loved ones. For the soldiers who are still in the battle zone serving their countries truly a miserable Christmas for them.

All shops will be decorated for this festive season, enticing consumers to spend more, the sad part is we are falling to this trap of commercial propaganda thus forgetting the real essence of Christmas. The way we celebrate Christmas will depend in our perspective and lifestyle. There is no right or wrong, but one thing is certain, Christmas time will always bring special family bonding with loved ones and friends.

My first Christmas in Australia in 1977 was a memorable one. We were residing at the Maribyrnong Hostel and some Filipino migrant families who had been in Australia before us had organised a Christmas party for us. We had delicious Filipino dishes, a Santa Claus giving gifts to our children. This alleviate our loneliness of spending Christmas away from home.

Regardless of age, gender, belief or lifestyle I suppose that LOVE and for Christian community, the celebration of the birth of CHRIST are the main reasons of what CHRISTMAS is all about.

My unpublished reflective thoughts
-----

God sometimes allowed us to have difficulties

In life

To suffer heartaches and sorrow

Not to punish us

But as a wake-up call

For us to realise we still need him

For Comfort and support

Hence making us a better

And stronger person than ever

# 15
## Change and Humility

Welcoming the new year to come, most of us will try once again to make changes in our lives, embracing the year ahead full of enthusiasm and anticipation wishing the new year will be much better than the previous one. With changes we need a lot of perseverance and motivation in order to do it effectively.

Change and humility are two words that go hand in hand. I do believe humility is the aftermath of every change that we do. It is the acceptance and acknowledgement of one's faults and flaws and how can one improve to be a better and stronger person

Reassessing your inner self is the best way to start. Begin with the easiest part that is achievable then do it one step at a time until you reach your goal. How-ever all these entail discipline and determination. The ideal and perfect way to change is not only to benefit ourselves but also for the welfare and interest of others, especially our loved ones. Nonetheless there are those people who are not open other's opinions, hence humility is beyond their perception and grasp.

Certainly, change is inevitable, circumstances will change as we go to different stages of our lives. Indeed, it is a part of growing up and moving on. Then again it is up to us to determine if the change is feasible to avoid disappointment and frustrations.

A sinner who is asking for forgiveness truly embodies the whole concept of humility, accepting their imperfections and mistakes and surrendering their love to our God Almighty.

Lastly a very good and ultimate example of humility was shown by Jesus. Although He is the son of God. He gave His life to redeem us from sins. He accepted the path of humility, humbled Himself, obedient even to the point of dying on the cross

An excerpt from my book
*My Innermost Thoughts*

### IMPERFECTION

That life does not need to be perfect
Imperfection, challenges, motivates, stimulates
The desire to grow and be a better person
Imperfection makes us humble
Helps us to accept things we can not change
Imperfection enables to see life
From a different perspective, and perhaps
We can see more in depth meaning of what life is all about

# 16
## Planning To Retire?

Retirement is the most crucial stage in our lives. It is dreaded by some, while others look forward for it. Are you well equipped and prepared for this? There are people who are planning for their retirement in five years or even more, but some times it does not matter how prepared you are. There are some unforeseen circumstances that are beyond your control, such as health issues and death. One has to be flexible when these tragic events occur.

Readjustment is one of the key issues taken into consideration when retiring. Suddenly you are with your partner 24/7 hence it can be quite a shock to both of you. Unfortunately as a result of this, some couples divorce during this time. This is the time for reassessing, compromising, reconnecting with each other. I truly believe that if both people are still in love with each other this issue will be easily resolved.

Yes it is true that financial freedom helps in retirement. However quite a lot of people were not fortunate enough to amass wealth upon retirement. Do not despair, as long as you have your wealth, loving and caring families and friends and you are at peace with yourself and GOD, happiness is achievable. These are the things money can not buy.

We are fortunate here in Australia that there are many organisations that help elderly and retirees. They have monthly events, programs and entertainment. There are lots of ways to enjoy retirement such as socialising with friends and joining that you have interest in. This is the time to explore your hidden talents for example learning new hobbies such as painting photography, work volunteer, writing and for those who can afford it, travelling overseas or visiting beautiful places in Australia.

When I retired seven years ago, I had the privileged of looking after my grandchildren. It was the most exhilarating experience in my life. I also found my passion for writing and music. To date I had published two books and currently have a third book, a novel underway. I have returned to studying intermediate piano and have joined several organisations, started to socialise with friends that I have not otherwise seen in decades. So who said retiring is boring? Definitely not me.

An excerpt from<br>
*My Innermost Thoughts*

I was often asked this question<br>
Are you bored retired?<br>
How do you fill up your time?<br>
I just smile<br>
Because I know within<br>
I am enjoying every minute being retired<br>
How can you be bored<br>
Sharing every moment with your loved ones?<br>
How can you be bored<br>
Exploring and reinventing yourself?<br>
How can you be bored doing things you are passionate about?<br>
Absolutely my colourful life begins during retirement

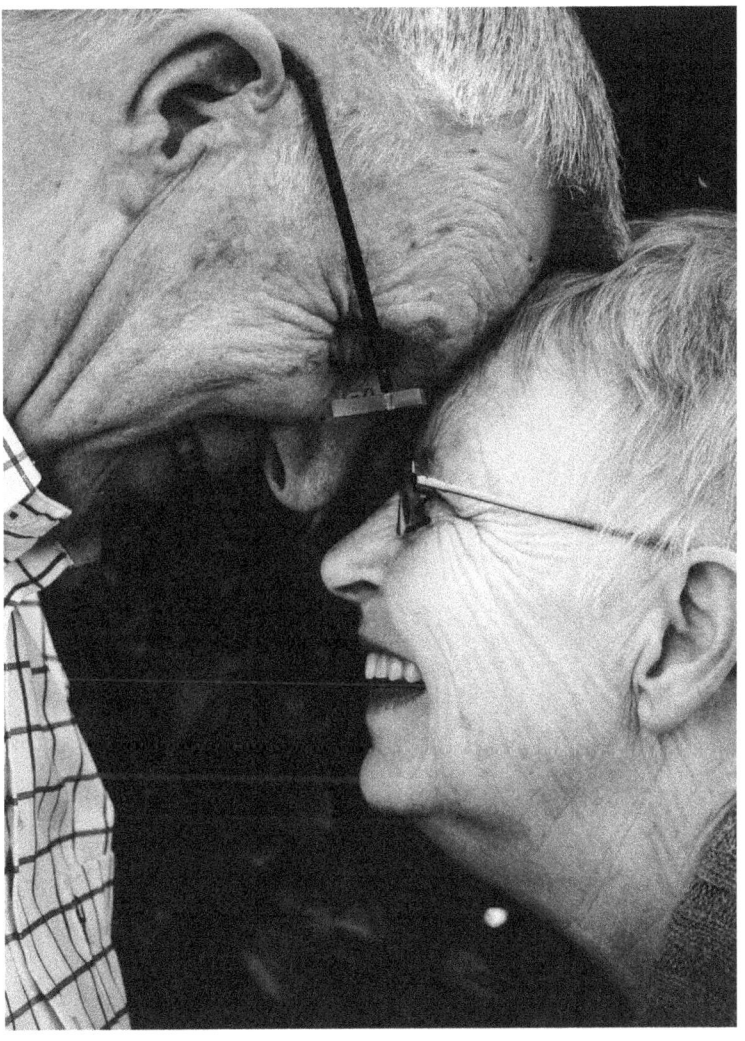

# 17
# The Eyes Say It All

What words fail to say, the eyes say it all; a quote from my second book My Passion My Calling. Our eyes are the reflections and revelations of our inner self and emotions that no one can hide. What we say at times is different from what we really mean and our eyes can express it more effectively than any words spoken, hence true to the popular saying that our eyes are a window of our soul.

A pretentious and fake smile can easily be seen through the eyes of a person. People forget that their eyes reveal how they feel. The feelings of happiness and surprise cause our eyes to get bigger and to light up, than when the feelings are of sadness and loneliness.

"Look me in the eye if you are telling the truth" is a popular statement to determine is lying or hiding something. Nonetheless. There are different reasons why some people do not feel comfortable having eye contact. Culture, anxiety, distress, shyness or just "in love" are amongst the reasons for avoiding eye contact.

At times in both mankind and animal kingdom an eye contact can pose a threat or a challenge that can endanger one's life. I know of a good looking guy who had a glance at a group of people and they followed him and beat him.

Criminal Minds one of my favourite television shows had mentioned that the eyes of psychopath and criminals have one thing in common;

their intense gaze and their emotions are empty and dull. Their eyes appear to be very different than the norms. On a more romantic scale, an emotional and touching movie scene I had seen recently was at the end of the movie *La La Land*, whereby no words were spoken between the two main characters. Only through their eyes, at a gaze, they connected and understood what their hearts and souls are saying. A powerful way of demonstrating how our eyes can be stronger than words.

Here is an Excerpt from my book<br/>
*My Innermost Thoughts*

Others hide their sorrows<br/>
Through their smiles<br/>
Others hide their fears<br/>
Through acting fearlessly<br/>
Others hide their insecurity<br/>
By acting superior to everyone<br/>
At times the things we see<br/>
Are not really what they are<br/>
There are more depth and meanings<br/>
To consider before judging others

# 18
## Love Conquers All

Just like the air we breathe that sustains our lives, yet we can not see it, love is something too intense to feel with our hears and souls but invisible to the human eye Love is the complete acceptance of someone who you care for and love, not who you want them to be. Love has no limits and it makes every moment of your life truly special. It is more potent than any lethal poison or venom known to man.

Love can divide nations and destroy families or friendship simply because it has no boundaries or rules to follow. Indeed it is quite difficult love as it is too complicated to fathom. It comes in many forms; the love of parents to their children, the divine love between people and GOD, the patriotic

One can not buy love, nor make someone love you, it can not be traded nor prevented. You can buy companionship, yet without love it is meaningless. Feeling in love is a surreal experience; you wont know when it will strike and at times it will catch you unprepared, akin to the saying "like a thief in the night". Hence it is the responsibility of both sides to be honest and trust worthy so that the relationship should be solid as a rock.

Love is freely given and should not be taken for granted by the recipient, so it will flourish and become stronger through the years

There is no such thing as a perfect marriage or relationship, but because of love for one another people will be able to resolve issues, or difficulties that can be detrimental to a relationship

Love is unconditional, forgiving, selfless, caring, inspiring but at times harmful and heartbreaking. I believe this is the highest form of human emotions. Almost all of us will choose love. A person without love and compassion within their hearts will never find the holy grail of happiness, contentment and the magical moments in life, that for me is not worth living for.

An Excerpt from my book
*My Passion My Calling*

Excuses will be made
Reason will be given
But
To show you care
And love someone
You do not need excuses
It should be manifested
In every way

# 19
# Miracles Do Exist

An Excerpt from my book
*My Innermost Thoughts*

Who said miracles don't exist anymore?
From the moment I open my eyes each morning
I see the sun shining in the sky
Or hear the sound of the rain
Pouring down on my roof
I see life in it
Beautiful creations from GOD
Enjoying the sun
Feasting from the pouring rain
Crops that we planted
Bearing its fruit
I see miracle in this
Indeed, about the harmonious relationship
Of nature and mankind
A simple thing I can say
Is the miracle of life

Each breath we take and each time we wake up are already miracles.

Our body is the symbol of the miracle of life. Cells inside our bodies change consistently at all times. Different organs inside interact with each other, each one of them having different functions to give us continuous life on earth. I believe that this is a living proof of daily occurrences of miracles, something beyond our comprehension of the intricate structures of the human body.

The vast solar system and how it works, every planet collaborates with one another in a movement in a predictable way I called this a *miracle*. To the sceptics, doubters, and non- believers, they can always provide technical explanation for this. Needless to say for us Christians and other religions we strongly believe that there is a greater force beyond our grasp that is responsible for all these things to happen.

Is it just only an urban myth when we hear stories of people being cured after prayer or somebody being diagnosed with cancer and given only few months to live survive that leaves doctors baffled?

One of the most popular miracles had occurred on the $13^{th}$ of October in 1917, in Fatima Portugal, witnessed by more than hundred thousand of people. It is the apparition of the Blessed Virgen Mary to the three shepherd children. According to many witnesses, after a period of rain, the dark cloud break and the sun appeared as an opaque spinning disk in the sky. It was well documented and the event was officially accepted as a miracle of the catholic church in October 13, 1930. How many times do we hear stories of babies and toddlers falling from a tall buildings and surviving? Would you consider this a miracle?

From my second book published in 2015 titled *My Passion My Calling* I described in the book the detailed story of my near-death experience and my first-hand encounter of the real essence of what a miracle was. After my recovery I developed a sudden passion in writing Inspirational Messages, a passion and desire that I did not have and feel before. I do believe I was given a second chance to live, to carry on a mission. To be able to help and reach people from all walks of life especially those who are confused, desperate and at their lowest ebb of their lives, through my inspirational writings.

This is the path that I have to follow and I am willing to do it as long as I am spiritually, physically and mentally capable. As I always say, sometimes a beautiful moment can happen and do not hesitate to follow it. Chase your dreams and most of all always chase your *destiny*.

# 20
## Forgiveness as a Virtue

The lord's prayer, a prayer thought by Jesus to his disciples, is now recited by all Christians. A beautiful prayer very inspiring and a meaningful passage one of which is: Forgive us our trespasses as we forgive those who trespass against us"

How many times do we pray The Lord's Prayer? Do we really digest and comprehend the quintessence of its meaning especially the part about forgiveness. Forgiving those who betrayed us and the degree of harm inflicted on us is not easy, but with sheer determination it will be achievable.

By forgiving you can move on and have closure. If there is still hatred in your heart, inner peace can not be found, thus it will haunt you forever. People who forgive are happier, healthier and have a good positive outlook of life. They are prepared to start a new beginning and and the experiences they endured will serve as a lesson, making them stronger and able to face the future with confidence.

There are people who will choose revenge over forgiveness. One form of revenge is not hurting your opponents physically, but destroying them internally watching them fall apart emotionally, mentally and spiritually. Will you feel better doing this? I do not think so, you will be worse than ever and you will make the situation more complicated. As a saying goes *"a mistake can not be corrected by another mistake"*.

Lenten season is a holy celebration for Christians all over the world. It is a time for fasting and repentance, a time for reflection when Jesus died on the cross. His first of His seven last words spoken on the cross was " *Father forgive them for they do not know what they are doing*" Even up to the last hour of his death, He was talking about forgiveness. The second time He mentioned forgiveness was during the repentance of a sinner beside him. A paramount manifestation of the virtue of forgiveness. The world would be more peaceful, joyous and better place if forgiveness will always reign in our hearts.

An excerpt from my book
*My Innermost Thoughts*

Letting it go
Does not mean forgetting the past
It is merely a preparation
For a new beginning
For a new life, for a new hope
Use your past as an inspiration
For a better future

# 21
## Journey of life

All of us have experienced different colourful stages in our lives, as we walk through the journey of life. Some are lucky to have a long journey of which they achieve fulfilment of their dreams, yet there are some who are unable to do so as they are taken by death prematurely.

At a very young age, the world, the world seems too big for our eyes. Everything around us is exciting and new to us. As we grow older our concepts of life change. The quest for knowledge becomes insatiable. We work hard for our ultimate desires, power and wealth. Then greed starts to slowly creep in and corrupts our body, mind and soul. But at the end of the journey we sometimes question ourselves: Is it all worth it?

At the prime time of our life, we think we are invincible, biting off more than we can chew. Keeping up with the modern times and keeping up with the joneses. But what really is a successful life? Is it measured by material possession or power? The answer will depend on your priorities in life. For me my priority is to have a relatively healthy body and a sound mind hence I can enjoy the rest of my journey.

Gaining experiences as we grow older makes us stronger, wiser and more compassionate. Why? Because our values change as we approach the end of our journey. What was relevant before is not now and is no longer important.

I had witnessed a very sad scenario that broke my heart. I was at the counter at a major grocery store and I overheard a son at his elderly mom: the mother had picked up the wrong item. In a soft tone of voice, she was telling her son that she could go back and change it. But the son angrily told her that he did not have time to wait for her.

Will this happen to me, will my loved ones treat me like this if I am no longer productive and strong? Scary thoughts indeed. Nonetheless, there are quite a lot of heart-warming scenarios; I had seen sons and daughters caring and looking after their elderly parents even bringing them to festivities and events, thus taking the time to share precious moments together. These will always put a smile on my face. I do hope my love ones will do the same for me and would never forget me in my old age…….. Well time will tell

### *Journey of Life*

In our younger days we were so eager
To learn new things, venture new experiences
Enjoy each time we went through
Extensive knowledge, we so desires
BUT,
It is in our mature years we can comprehend
Understand, appreciate
Appreciate everything we learned
And all the experiences as we
Walk through the Journey of life

# 22
# Mothers, The Most Loved People On Earth

I believe our life's journey starts in our mother's womb. Mothers giving us all the nourishment needed making us stronger by the day. After nine months, a mother will give the most precious gift to the world: a new born child.

The cutting of the umbilical signifies the physical separation of a mother and a child. However the connection and bonding continues. The baby still needs nourishment from the first day he/she was born with the mother giving breast milk to her baby. Indeed the child can feel a mother's first touch hugs and kisses and the warm caring love she gives.

The profound love of a mother to her children can never be fathomed. It defies logic and reasonable explanations. An example of unconditional love, a love that is full of sacrifices and caring.

Its not only human who manifested our love for our offspring, but also to the animal kingdom. One documentary I saw on TV, a scene that really touches my heart, showed a big cat protecting her new born from predators, diverting the attention from her newborn resulting in herself becoming a victim or a casualty. A pinnacle example of what a mother's love is.

A face that only a mother can love is an expression. A saying that epitomises the overall description of a mother's love to her children.

There is a strong connection of love, trust, and intensity between a child and their mother. The influence of a mother to her children is very significant in the process of their development. As shown by the overwhelming scientific and psychological studies. Children that are well loved are mostly self- confident, happy and have a good positive outlook on life.

So let us not celebrate Mother's Day only once a year, but everyday as a recognition of their role in moulding, loving and all the sacrifices they do for their children.

An excerpt from my book
*My Passion My Calling*

A Mother's Heart
*A mother's heart is so strong*
*It can withstand all the pain*
*Sorrows and heartaches*

*A mother's heart will always*
*Forgive*
*No matter what*
*A mother's love will always give*
*Even if there is no more left to give*
*One can not fathom a heart*
*Of a mother*
*Unless you are a mother*

# 23
## Thanks for the Memories

Each year will come and go, and at the end of each year we are always in the process of preparing, assessing and evaluating the things we had done and had happened in our lives. There are memories that can be forgotten but there are some that can linger on forever and will always make us happy.

Both pleasant and painful memories can happen for the past year, and for the unfortunate ones, this is the time to move on and try to embrace the coming year with hope, new life and a new beginning. From the past mistakes we can now set up new goals and aspirations. For grieving families who lost loved ones, remember to concentrate for the living loved ones who still need your care and support.

It is no use having a long list of New Year's resolution. Based from statistic only 8% people will keep their New Year's resolution. Nonetheless remember that the choices we made will create and shape our future.

Be practical and sensible when making a resolution, start with the easiest one, take baby step and when you feel you are ready you can set or aim for your next goal. By doing this it won't create disappointment and frustrations.

Prioritise what is important, but consider as well that your changes will benefit not only yourself but your loved ones. Ask you family for support if needed and I am sure they will always be there for you.

I am truly thankful for the memories for the past year. It was the year that we celebrated our 50th wedding anniversary, the same year I had launched my 3rd book and my first novel "Moments of Love, Lust and Ecstasy. The previous year I decided to continue my piano study and fortunate enough to pass the Australian Music Examination Board for intermediate level.

This time I won't be making any New Year's Resolution instead I will continue my passion for writing, music and supporting my Charity.

Thanks for the outgoing years for all the wonderful memories I had and I hope next year ahead will be the same or better for me and for all of us.

Excerpt from my book
*My Innermost Thoughts*

*It is the choice we make in our lives*
*That makes life itself*
*Full of challenges and surprises*
*Hence shaping and creating*
*Our journey of life*

# 24
## Divine Intervention

There are so many things in our lives that can happen without logical explanations. For sure atheist and non-believers will always have their doubts. They will have technical explanations then hide their frustrations once they run out of reasons. " A *blip or glitch of the system*" will be used as their explanation. They refused to accept that miracles do exist. I do believe in miracles and a Divine Intervention.

What is really a Divine Intervention? According to Google, it is a miracle or an act of God that causes something good to happen or stop something bad happening.

I am no stranger to this kind of phenomenon, and will gladly share my eerie experienced we had last New Year's-eve in 2017. My landline was not working for the last three months. I can call but we can not receive incoming calls. We were about to leave at 5:30 pm going to the city and the phone rings. At long last the phone was working again. It was a call from a friend inviting us to celebrate and welcome the coming year at their house. I told her to hang up and call again. This time it did not work. Requested few friends to call us but with negative results.

We visited our loved ones in the city, spent precious time bonding with them then we left around 10:30 pm to go to my friend's house to welcome the coming year with full of hope for a better year to come. So much enjoyed the party that it was already 2:30 am when we decided to go home. As we opened the door the house was fully lighted, ransacked and like a war zone. The robbers entered the back door of the laundry room. , and a bolo Machete from the laundry was taken and could be used to hurt or even killed both of us. Valuables, computers, designer bags etc were taken. Material things can be replaced, and it was a blessing we were not hurt.

Both of us were traumatised about the incident. We were lucky we were not at home when the home invasion happened. Just one phone call from a phone that was defective saves our lives. My new phone provider cannot give technical explanation why I was able to receive an incoming call that afternoon. He said: Probably a glitch in the system.

I do not think so. I personally think this is one good example of a Divine Intervention. I was given again a third chance of life. My second chance of life was fully discussed in detailed from my second book *My Passion My Calling*. Being angry with them will not change what had happened. I feel sorry for their lost souls and I pray may they find the right path of direction to follow.

Because of this incident it gave me an unequivocal assurance of strength, confidence to follow "HIS" calling; that is; to continue and fulfil my mission of promoting: Love, Peace, Compassion through my books and written articles and I will continue doing this, with the best that I can offer.

An excerpt from my book
*My Passion My calling*

---

Once we had gone through trials and tribulations
The more we appreciate the real essence
Of what life is all about.
It is not just living our lives
But it is all about how we live
Our lives on earth

# B. Reflections

# A. Poems

1. **SEASONS OF LIFE**

   In every stage in life we had
   In every journey and experience we had
   For every hardship, sorrow and pain
   There will always be an end
   Just like the winter cold and woeful
   Spring will always follow
   Alive and blissful
   Forgetting the dark, miserable winter nights
   And moving to a bright new life
   For a fresh beginning and a new way of life

2. **FINDING LOVE**

   Being in love we start
   To rediscover our inner- self
   And the real meaning of what
   Life is all about
   Finding love is magical
   Moments and precious time
   We shared with someone
   We truly love and adore
   Finding Love is priceless

3. **HAPPINESS**
    Happy are those who can forgive
    Because they will find peace
    Within and others
    Happy are those who stay - connected
    With HIM
    It's the only way to eternal - salvation
    Happy are those who are willing to share
    And help others
    Because they can make a difference
    In this troubled -world
    We live in
    Happy are those who can love
    And accept people
    Because they will be able to love and be loved

4. **A SONG OF LOVE**
    I cannot count the number
    Of the stars in the sky
    But I can see its brightness
    Beauty and grandeur
    I cannot fathom the depth
    Of the deep blue sea
    But I can feel its serenity
    Calmness and tranquillity
    It's the same as
    I cannot tell you
    How much I love you

But I can feel within my heart
The depth and intensity
Of my love for you

5. **MY ORDEAL**

So much pain and sorrow I feel
Akin to a sword or dagger
Slowly piercing through my heart
Dissecting it to pieces
At times I thought
I died a thousand times
Then each time bouncing back to life
Fighting as hard as I can
Wishing to overcome all these
Please help me God

6. **THE POWER OF LOVE**

Love encompasses everything
Does not know its boundaries
It is so strong and powerful
It will conquer everything
Along its path
Does not care who you are
Regardless of gender, status or beliefs
Makes a strong man cries
And a weak man strong

7. **ABOUT LIFE**
   One should to know when to stop
   One should know to call it quits
   But then again
   One should know when to start
   All over again
   Timing plus luck are an important roles
   In doing it efficiently and effectively

8. **DECEIT AND HONESTY**
   Deceit and honesty are always with us
   Since time immemorial
   These are the reasons
   Why we have conflicts
   Amongst Nations and people
   Indeed- a harsh realities of life
   All of us can make a difference
   If we start to practice the virtue
   Of compassion, love and tolerance
   For one another

9. **ETERNAL FLAME**
   One of the sweetest things in life
   Is to be able to share moments
   With your love ones up to the
   Last journey of your life
   To be able to look back together
   Those beautiful and unforgettable memories

To be able to grow old together
Learning to accept each -others
Faults and shortcomings
To be able to let the flame of love
We always cherish be
Forever in our hearts
Will remain as passionate forever.

10. **THE FOUNTAIN OF YOUTH**

Most of us are always seeking
The fountain of youth
Yet our spiritual nourishment
Seems to be for-granted
Everybody wants power and fame
Yet few people are fighting for a cause
Fighting for the oppress
Few are taking actions and solutions
For all- the humanitarian problems
We do face globally

11. **THE POWER OF MUSIC**

Such mystical, magical influence
In anyone's life
It eases, changes and affect
Our emotions and moods
Does alleviate and relieve
Whatever sorrows, heartaches we have
At times bring back beautiful

Memories of past years gone by
Thanks for the musician, composers, and singers
Who bring colours to our lives
Through the majestic moving sound of MUSIC

# B. Inspirational Thoughts and Messages

**1**

People always love the underdogs
They will always sympathise for them
A good quality of us
However — once the underdogs bounce back
Thrive in their new-found success and fame
    Surpassing sympathisers
That's the start of bigotry, indifferences and conflicts

**2**

It is easier to understand rocket science
Than the complexity and intricacy
Of human minds, thoughts and emotions

**3**

Pain and hurt will be needed
To make us humble, a wake- up call
Realising that
We still need HIM for strength and support

**4**

God sometimes allowed us
To have difficulties in life
Not to punish us
But to remind us
We still need Him
Hence making us a better
And stronger person than ever.

**5**

We came to this earth alone
Through our journey
We were able to create happy families
Beautiful friendship and memories
At the end we leave the world alone

**6**

The illusion that we created
At times brings joy
Or heartfelt anguish and sorrow
Especially when the expectations
And the realisations, that all things
Will -come to an end.

**7**
We tend to be a prisoner of our own self
Remembering past experiences
Too scared to move on
To let it go
Conquering with fear one's
Mind and soul
We always blame others, destiny and fate
Giving excuses for our failures
Failing to accept our own inadequacies

**8**
The season of Winter is akin to the darkest moments of our lives
Unforeseen - traumatic tragedies will happen
As long you have a solid faith in God
And the support of loved ones and friends
You can overcome all your predicaments.
Soon Spring will be around
New hope, new beginning
Our journey will be rosier and joyful
Than ever

**9**
Whatever we do
Whatever the outcome will be
If we did it with
Dignity and passion
That's all that matters
Its- only a start of a challenge
Let all our experiences be our guide
And all the things we learned
From our journey
With the right focus and determinations
Success is within our reach

**10**
Once you conquer your fear
There is no turning back
The only way is to move forward
Then the smell of success
Is imminent and reachable

**11**
At times out of desperation we do things
Hurting not only ourselves
But people around us
Loved ones, friends and families
They are the people you will need for support
And strength

## 12

Once or few times in our lives
We made crucial decision
That can change the path
Of our life's journey
This is challenge, without it
You cannot improve and
Dreams will be unreachable

## 13

Truth hurts but one should have
The courage to face it
In- order to move on
Tomorrow will be brighter than
The past and the present

## 14

Yes, we do receive all the blessings
    From HIM
But are we willing to share all these
    To the less fortunate?

## 15

It is in our own weakness that
We desperately tried to hide
Yet we easily judge others
Their imperfections and shortcomings

**16**

We will be able to improve and, analyse
Our own imperfections
By knowing the imperfections
And mistakes of others

**17**

The art of listening has a lot of advantages
You will be able to analyse
And read between the lines
What people are trying to hide or convey
An effective way of getting through
Their inner thoughts

**18**

If each one of us will do an act
Of kindness even once in your life
The world will be a perfect place
To live

**19**

Envy is akin to a poison
Creeping our body
Slowly polluting our mind body and soul
Saddest part is the person is not even aware of it

**20**

In time of troubles and tribulations
We seek and remember "HIM'
Do we still connect, and pray to "HIM"
In time of abundance and glorious
Joyful moments?

**21**

I believe each one of us has a mission
    On Earth
To follow "HIS" teachings
To use our talent bestowed to us
In the best possible ways
To help; share, and serve others
There are those who use their talents
For greed, power and - eventually
Will end up to their own
Self- Destruction

**22**

Life is full of surprises and regardless
Of what they are we should always
Be prepared and flexible
And be able to cope everything
That cross our path
Lucky are those who have support
From families and friends
But think of those
Who got no one to turn to

**23**

Deep within you know you had not changed
It's the people around you had
Sometimes it does hurt that old friends
Though not all of them, failed to support you
New found friends are the ones who did.
Do not be disappointed. Continue achieving
Your goals in life. Always remember do not expect
To please everyone. Look after yourself first
No one will do it for you

**24**

There are people who will give
More than they have
While they are those
Who will get more than
They should

**25**

I do believe that the character of a person
Will be greatly manifested
On how they treat another person
Regardless of their status in the community
And for what - they can do for you

**26**

Lucky are those people who were given
    A second chance
To rectify their mistakes
To be able to change their journey
    Of life

**27**

Age should not be a barrier
In chasing and following one's dreams
It is the passion in our hearts
That will make us truly alive
And looking forward for tomorrow's blissful
Journey and challenges

**28**

The more you had experienced
Heartaches and sorrows
The more you can transcend effectively
Your thoughts, ideas and emotions
In your writings

**29**

No one should ever sacrifice
Their happiness, because of the
Pressure from society, friends
Or even families

**30**

There is no need to run away
From something that is important
And matters to you
Just to please others
Always remember to follow
Your heart - that will lead you
To the right direction

**31**

Sometimes and most of the time
The anticipations are more agonising
Than the actual results
Or event that will happen

**32**

You would think that your life
    Is perfect
Till one day there are things
Happened beyond your control
Whatever they are we have
To learn to accept it
Just count your blessings for
All the things you still have

**33**
In love we rediscover
Our inner self
And the real meaning of
What life is all about
Love teaches us to be humble
Love teaches us to be forgiving
To be sensitive and compassionate

**34**
Often you will realise your priceless
Possessions are the least
Expensive ones
Enjoy and make the most of
What you have
Than complain of what
You do not have

**….35**
Always treasure and cherish
The company of loved ones
And friends while you still can

**36**
Let no hate, greed and jealousy
Reign in our hearts
Or you will not find peace forever

**37**

Make each day a celebration
    Of Life
A life full of hope
A life full of positive attitude
Negativity will always
Produce stress and unhealthy
For the mind and soul

**38**

It is not enough to say the word
    "I Love You"
To your loved ones
It must be be manifested by actions
Or else the words will be meaningless

**39**

If Passion becomes an obsession
Followed by greed. It will turn a person
To a monster. He will destroy everything
Along the way
No matter what would be the consequences

**40**

People will always forget what you say
People will never forget
How you treat them
And how you make them feel

**41**

The saddest part of one's life
Is living without love
Alienated with others
They are too busy working success, wealth
    And fame
At the end it is too late, finding themselves
Alone and miserable
    Is it worth it?

**42**

People around you and the
Environment you grew up
Will have a great influence and impact
It will shape what you will
Likely to be in the future

**43**

Always be happy and do not worry
Too much about what others will say
Follow your heart
Avoid negativity
Think positive and you will get
Positive results

**44**

The sacrifices we do for our children
To give them a better future
Will be always our priority
Though we are not expecting
Anything in return
It is still nice to be acknowledged
By them for everything we did.

**45**

Music   Heals the souls
    So Powerful
It somehow affects us
In so many different
    Ways

**46**

It is not about what you want to be
It is all about What you are meant to be
That's when Destiny takes full control

**47**
However intense the pain
    We felt
Grieving for the death of loved ones
We should to remember, we are only
Temporary residence on this world
Life should go on until the day
It is our turn to leave
And will come face to face
With our creator

**48**
Denial is your utmost enemy and hindrance
For your success, progress and growth
Though it is quite difficult to change
Do one step at a time
Until you succeed

**49**
When the music stops
And the laughter had vanished
That is the time you will realised
And know who your real friends are

**50**

Being open minded about
Everything in life is quite
Brain stimulating
You become more tolerance
Accommodating and non-judgemental
And be able to relate to everyone

**51**

We are all different That makes life interesting
Just imagine if we are all the same
Life will be very boring

**52**

It will be impossible to change a person
At least what we can do is
To give them something
To think about

**53**

It takes a person with integrity and honesty
To say I am sorry. While it takes a fool and
Self – centred person to deny
And accept
Their mistakes

**54**

Nowadays we are more conscious
Of our physical Image than
Our spiritual needs
A sign of the modern times

**55**

So sad there are people even at the
Last moments of their lives
Still show bitterness, discontentment
Hence   peace -within themselves
And others were never achieved

**56**

The beauty of nature never ceases to amaze me
Who said Miracles do not exist anymore?
Just look around you
And you will find the answers

**57**

One should not stop improving thyself
Regardless of age, gender
This what makes life more interesting
And more reasons and inspirations
To live

**58**

We keep on searching endlessly
But at the end we soon realised
The most prized possessions are the
Least expensive ones and at times for free

**59**

Anyone can do the things their heart desires
It is just a matter of sheer perseverance
Hard - work and the determination
To make it happen

**60**

We need to stop and question ourselves
Is it all worth it?
All the hassles, pressure from work
Keeping up with modern times
To be the best of the things we do
Denying ourselves with the - needed break
To spend special - moments with the loved ones
Friends? At the end you will realised
You can not bring back those wasted years
It is too late. You ended up miserable and
Discontented as ever.

**61**

There will be moment in our lives that we
Had reached our lowest ebb. The support
Of our families and friends are the only
Way to keep us going, giving us strength
To face life challenges and above all
Our faith in "Him" will give us the hope
We so desire.

**62**

Quest for knowledge is never ending
The desire for adventure, calculated risks
Are amongst the spices of life

**63**

Being aware always of what is going on around you
Being focused will give you the edge
To be upfront from your competitors
Truly a recipe for success for all
Professionals and entrepreneurs

**64**

It does not take too much effort
To do an act of kindness
Yet there are people who chose
To inflict pain and misery to others

**65**

A smile can do wonders
It can mean a lot of things
It denotes friendship peace
Appreciation and kindness

**66**

Appreciate even the smallest things
Of what you have
Enjoy all your blessings day by day
Always hope that the best things
In your life still will come
Staying positive is the way to live

**67**

Controlled risk is much better
Than not taking risk at all
One way you can achieve success

**68**

Love, Understanding, compassion
Are three beautiful traits
You can give to all fellowmen

**69**

Pretending to be what you are not
Will not get you anywhere
It will only add on to your frustrations

And at the end It will complicate
Your life and deepens your insecurity

**70**

You do not have to prove anything
To anyone. You are what you are
They should accept you as you are
And not what they want you to be

**71**

Accepting criticism is the way
You can evaluate, improve
And re assessing oneself

**72**

It is how you perceive life
That can make or unmake a person
The choices we made can shape
Our future and the path of the journey
Of your life you want to follow

**73**

Each one of us is special
That is how "HE" created us
It is up for us to find it
To believe in our self
Continue searching and following
Your dreams

**74**

Beautiful expression of oneself
One's emotions and powerful lyrics
Soul moving melodies
Can be felt by all of us
Through the magical sound of music

**75**

We always do not appreciate
Things we already have
We keep on searching and searching
For the holy grail of happiness
Until one day we realised
It is already within us all the time

**76**

Angels do not need wings
You can be an angel
By reaching and help others
Each one of us can make a difference

**77**

Let not grieving overtake your mind
Body and soul. Connecting with HIM
Through prayers and meditation
Can ease the pain you feel
Remember there are people
Who still love and care for you

**78**

I wonder what will be my life
Without the love of families and friends
My soul will be empty Then living
Will be miserable and lonely

**79**

It is the thought of a permanent or temporary
Separations from our loved ones
Can make us feel unhappy or grieving
Hence creating a big impact in our lives
And at times permanent hole in our hearts
That will take many years to mend
And sometimes it will never heal

**80**

I do believe, no matter what you become
Do not forget your root
Where you came from
    AND
The people who helped you
Become of what you are today

**81**
Few times in my life
That I got frustrated
Because things did not happen
>My Way

And I started to question
Why me?
At the end I realised that it had to happen
For my own benefit
I do believe for every predicament encountered
There will always be a silver lining ahead

**82**
At the twilight years of our lives
We realised that these are the most
Important factors in life:
>Health
>Inner peace
>Families and friends
>Food and shelter

All the rest will only be secondary

**83**
All actions are done with intentions
And motivations
Quite a few times we failed to recognise
Analyse and understand the aftermath of it.

**84**

Those who suffered the most
Will know and appreciate
The value and the real essence
Of what happiness is all about.

**85**

Power and greed when combined
Will be so lethal and addictive
Akin to the most dangerous drugs and substance
Known to mankind
The havoc they will produce
Will be mind- blowing

**86**

I feel closer to my Creator
Each time I am in my garden
Digging the soil, planting trees and flowers
Or just admiring the beauty of nature
Whenever or wherever I maybe

**87**

At times we do not allow
Love, understanding and compassion
Reign and flourish in our hearts
Because we are focus on ourselves
And let greed and hunger for power
Prevail within

**88**

It is not about being passionate
On what you believe
It is all about doing what
You believe into actions

**89**

Regardless of what had happened
Regardless of what reasons they are
One must face life with courage
Continue to move on
Just for the sake of all the people
Who still love and care for you

**90**

Maturity begins when you start
To accept and respect people
As they are and not what you
Want them to be

**91**

When love grows
Amidst all the hatred and chaos
It becomes more powerful
Intense and meaningful

**92**

Love will always find
And makes its way
No matter when where
And how

**93**

You shall never presume
You are the best
Because someone, somewhere
Will be better than you

**94**

The hurt is more intense
      And painful
When it comes from someone
You love, trusted and cared for

**95**

One's life experiences
Enhances your knowledge
Strengthen one's character
And served one's guiding light
As one's walk through
The journey of life

**96**
Who are we to judge others
Where our own imperfections
We just ignore and do nothing
About it

**97**
There is nothing more gratifying
Than to see your family
Eating with gusto
From the labour of love
Of the food you cooked
And prepared for them

**98**
Regardless of what people will say
Regardless of what people will think
    About you
If you really believe in what you do
You should go on and push through
These are only one of the many things
You will encounter
In achieving your dreams

**99**

I believe the real and true happiness
Can only be achieved
By sharing special moments
With loved ones, families and friends

**100**

Time is the master of our lives
Brutal unforgiving, relentless
Waste it
Then suffer the consequences
Time can never be taken back
Nor can be retrieved

**101**

No matter how fast you run
Darkness will always follow you
You got the choice confronting
Your demon
Or forever be a prisoner of yourself
And peace within can never be found

**102**
There will always be a thin line
Between obsession and passion
Once it starts to frustrate you
And the continuous craving
For the ultimate desire for success and fame
That is where obsession is taking over your passion
Hence it will create detrimental consequences
On your values, spiritually and morally
It will change the way you perceive life

**103**
Simple lessons in life:
It is always best to have moments of evaluation
Assessment and recollection of the
Things happening in your life
Do make priorities of what is important
Concentrate more on people
Who care, love and support you
Who will be there for you
Regardless of the situation
Disconnect to those who don't
Do not be affected with criticism
Instead use them for your own advantage
Hence making you a better and stronger person

**104**

True love lingers on
Even up to the last breath of your life
All sacrifices will turn into glory
Just for the sake of the people
You adore and love

**105**

Though at times expectation
Can bring heartaches and pain
Without it
We do not have the motivation and inspiration
To follow and chase your dreams

**106**

It is not only saying
In words you love someone
But it is all about caring and even
Sacrificing if needed
For someone you are deeply in love

**107**

One cannot fully appreciate
The sweet glory of success
Until you gone through failures
Trials and hardship along the way
One can- not achieve peace happiness
And serenity in life
If greed, envy and jealousy
Existed in your heart
One can -not fully fathom
The joy of living
Until you open your heart
Giving yourself a chance
To love and be loved

**108**

Growing up to an adult
Does not mean
You are invulnerable
To all evils that always
Existed in this world

**109**

Wondering what tomorrow will bring?
I just go on moving forward
Till I will reach my goal
Till success will be achieve
That is what life is all about

**110**

Just one moment that had happened
    In your life
Your perspective in life
Will have a complete turnaround
Change will be inevitable
Past dreams won't be feasible
You start to think of different
Alternatives in the future

# PONDERING THOUGHTS

Lorna Ramirez

Published in Australia by Lorna Ramirez
First published in Australia February 2018
This edition published 2019
Copyright © Lorna Ramirez 2019
Cover design, typesetting: WorkingType Studio

The right of Lorna Ramirez to be identified as the Author of the Work has been asserted in accordance with the Copyright, Designs and Patents Act 1988.

All rights reserved. No part of this publication may be reproduced, stored in a retrieval system, or transmitted, in any form or by any means without the prior written permission of the publisher, nor be otherwise circulated in any form of binding or cover other than that in which it is published and without a similar condition being imposed on the subsequent purchaser.

Ramirez, Lorna
*Pondering Thoughts*
PBK: 978-0-6482130-6-2
EBOOK: 978-0-6482130-7-9
pp114

# Acknowledgements

Special Thanks to Alyssa Cary
my Personal Assistant

**Dedicated To**

My loving husband, Claro
Grandchildren Alyssa and Amelia
Children and their partners:
Carlo and Marie
Maria and Steve
My sister Victoria Polon

# 1
# Of Human and Divine Love

*"Loving someone does not mean you love "GOD" less"* A meaningful and touching phrase explained by the Mother Superior to Maria from the movie *The Sound of Music*. Indeed, it is true that many are called but few are chosen. Love is like a thief in the night, it can strike anyone without warning

I am truly blessed to experience both divine and human love. In my late teens I felt the blissful happiness of divine love. In that moment, praying was another realm of my spiritual soul which transformed me to find a joyful connection with "God". I found complete serenity and tranquillity with him. Praying in the church gave me an unexplained exultation that enveloped my body and soul.

Every Sunday I would spend the whole day at the church doing church activities, and having religious meetings. It is at this point that my parents began to get worried that I might follow the footsteps of my cousins who entered the monastery.

Then someone had touched my innocent and fragile heart, I cried, prayed and asked why me? He was a young seminarian who was soon to be an ordained priest . No words were spoken between us, but our body language, smiles and the expressions of our eyes said it all. I was confused and felt a different kind of love.

Of course I attended his ordination, and shook his hands to

congratulate him after the ceremony. He squeezed my hands tightly and with a tender tone in his voice he said " I am sorry". I replied in a small voice as I looked down unable to meet his gaze I said " I understand"

Moving on I concentrated on my studies and finished my B.S in Chemical Engineering, then, was lucky to get a job as an industrial chemist in a textile industry where I met my husband.

Out of the blue one Sunday evening at a restaurant, I bumped in to the priest. I broke the news to him that I would be getting married in the next few months. He graciously offered his service to be the officiating priest. And I gladly accepted .

At the wedding reception he asked me , if I was happy with the love that I had found. I quickly responded and with a smile on my face" I said "I am very happy." That was the last time I saw him.

I have no regrets with my life now. I have husband who is very supportive in all my passions and even cares to all my whims and caprices. A husband who loves me so dearly. , with whom I raised two successful children and have two wonderful grandchildren. I could not ask for more

I firmly believe, whatever love you choose, be it love to family,, priests, missionaries , soldiers , country or God they are all the same, they take and give us dedication, commitment and responsibility.

An excerpt from my book,
*Innermost Thoughts*

At times we cry within
Yet no one can hear
The pain and heart, only you can feel
Those shattered dreams and memories of yesteryears
That haunt you vividly as only they can
But That was then and today is different
Years have passed and things have changed
Once again, Triumphantly you emerge now
A better stronger person

# 2
## Perfect Imperfection

TO BE PERFECT IS TO BE IMPERFECT. What is imperfection? It is a fault, flaw, a disfigurement distorted, and the descriptive lists go on and on. Imperfection will always be abhorred by many. A lot of us will aim and desire for perfection in everything we do. However there are lessons to be learned for being imperfect. We can as well learned from the mistakes of others, and make these work for your own advantage.

Imperfections inspire us to be creative, to be strong, and compassionate. A pianist will endure hours of practice each day to overcome his imperfection and to achieve perfection in playing classical pieces with ease and confidence. A rough diamond will be turned into an exquisite expensive stone desired by many., thanks to the creative skilled hands of a diamond cutter. An aspiring chef, will diligently work to perfect their own signature dish. These are only a few examples how imperfection can lead to perfection.

Imperfection challenges us to work harder to reach your ultimate goal and be the best of what you are. Imperfection makes us compassionate and fully understand the feelings and suffering of other people especially who share the same problems you are going through.

Nonetheless there are also an ugly side of being a perfectionist.

Being a perfectionist will lead to stress, mental blackout, and at times depression. Being a perfectionist you doubt other people abilities, thus unable to delegate the work and the end result will be discontentment ., unhappiness and exhaustion.

How can we deal with imperfections?..... There are several ways to deal with Imperfections, first and foremost we should remember that no one is perfect. We all have our own shortcomings and flaws.

Secondly just enjoy life itself, and if you have physical disabilities, try to overcome them by adjusting what is comfortable with your situations. There are those people with no legs and arms but still live normal life by conquering their own challenges and becoming more than they could imagine. Know your limitations and explore your talents especially for those with physical disabilities. They can be good in sport, writing, and music.

Do not compare yourself with others, as It can lead to disappointments, and frustrations. Each of us is different and special in our own way. Imagine if we lived in a perfect world with perfect people around, life will be boring and uninteresting. Always count your blessings and this will put a smile on your face.

I believe that once you reach your goal of being nearly perfect in life whether it be a success in career, financial status, fame family, we must always remain humble as we can or else perfection is irrelevant.

Excerpt from
*Reflective Contemplations*

---

I believe that life does not need to be perfect
Imperfection Challenges, motivates, stimulates
The desire to grow and be a better person
Imperfection makes us humble
Helps us to accept, things we can not change
Imperfection enables us to see life
From a different perspective
Perhaps so, we can see more in depth meaning
Of what life is all about

# 3
## Pondering Thoughts

*Heard melodies are sweet but those unheard are sweeter,* an excerpt from Ode On A Grecian Urn written by the romantic poet John Keats. This is one of my favourite poems. There are so many interpretations of this verse and my own is of someone you are so much in love with and words are not enough to express your feelings, but when manifested with actions such as the sacrifices you are willing to do for your loved ones, it will be more potent than all the descriptive words spoken.

The first week of September is the celebration of Father's Day and I dedicate this article for all the fathers in the world. Most fathers are subdued in expressing their emotions, however they will always do whatever it takes to protect their families from all unexpected events and predicaments They appear to be strong and a disciplinarian. In actuality, deep within they have a soft spot for their children especially their daughters. Arguably Fathers are the foundation of a family unit but of course with the help of mothers. Fathers have a major role in the development of their children. Children who have a wholesome relationship with their fathers, grow up to be a well balances and happy responsible adults.

In today's environment, fathers have a myriad role in the family. They are not only seen as a bread winner but also take an active part in household chores and the upbringing of their children. Every Father's Day, I always remember my Dad. Like the verse in the Ode On A Grecian Urn, my father is a man of few words. Yet his heart was as big as the universe and beyond. He had helped his brothers and sisters as well as my mom's brothers and sisters to be able to finish their university degrees in Manila. He was a person who will give his last money in his pocket to anyone asking for help.

I still remember his smile, that was warm as the morning sun, his laughter was so infectious like the sound of the echo of the roaring seas. His eyes will sparkle like the stars in the sky of happiness every time he was surrounded with loved ones, families and friends. His generosity, kindness and joyous nature continue to resonate with me, thus having an impact and tremendous influence in all my writings. I love and miss you DAD……. Really I Do

Excerpt from
*Reflective Contemplations*

It is not enough to say the word
"I LOVE YOU"
To your loved ones
It Must be manifested by actions
Or else the words will be meaningless

# 4
# Winter Season in Our Lives

There will always be a Winter Season in our lives regardless who you are, and no one can be spared.

Just like cold and dreary season of winter, there are times in our lives that winter falls upon us through the loss of loved ones, loss of a friend, health issues, job loss or the end of a relationship. It will be the lowest ebb in our lives.

For some it can be manageable , they can survive the season and they can re-assess, reflect and move on. Sadly others just can not cope, that which will be detrimental for their health and can at times result to family breakdown

My friend from overseas couldn't cope or come to terms with the loss of their first born child. Depression, and failing health slowly overtaking her body and soul. Supports from families and friends seemed futile and she saw no reason to live ., because of the unfortunate situation, her husband left her, and that only added to her misery. And resulted in her ending her own life.

I truly believe that "GOD" should be our refuge in times of our troubles and heartaches. At times your strong faith in "HIM" through prayers will help and guide you and through this you can find your inner strength to overcome all the obstacles in life.

A gardener will always plan, prepare, and improve his garden in preparation for the coming Spring Season. It is the time for a gardener to plant new beautiful bulbs, bare rooted roses for an exquisite display of colourful flowers in Spring and Summer Seasons. Trees, fruit trees with no leaves an eye sore to us will be transformed into arrays and display of different magnificent dazzling colours in Spring and Summer.

Akin to a gardener, Winter season in our lives will be the time for contemplation, meditation, planning , learning the lessons from our mistakes, failures and an eye opener.. It can be a guiding light for a better future, because after all, Spring will follow and this will be the beginning of a new life, new hope for a brighter tomorrow. We need winter season in our lives to truly appreciate more the joy of having Spring and Summer seasons in our lives.

Excerpt from
*Reflective Contemplations*

### SEASONS OF LIFE

In every stage in life we had
In every journey and experience we had
For every hardship, sorrow and pain
There will always be an end
Just like Winter cold and woeful
Spring will always follow
Alive and blissful
Forgetting the dark miserable Winter night
And moving to a bright new life
For a fresh beginning and a new way of life

# 5
## The Wheel Of Life

Goodbye for the past year and welcome to the coming year.. Another year has gone and we are a year older and wiser. This is a time for soul searching, reflection, and reassessment of things to do to make the coming year better, rosier and more successful than the year before.

It seems only yesterday that my family celebrated our very first New Year in Australia. That was forty years ago, and in those days 'celebrations of Christmas and New year were very subdued; a far cry from todays environment or compared to what it is today,

As migrant in the late 70's we worked hard, hence we were able to buy our first home. As the children were growing up and the prospect of my parents in laws coming to Australia to live with us, we moved to a bigger house in a nearby suburb. It was a quiet courtyard. Our neighbours were mostly pensioners and retirees. We were one of the youngest families in the area. In those days we bonded with our neighbours and at times participated in street celebrations for Christmas and New Year.

As time passed by, most of them had gone to the nursing home or passed away. Now we have became the oldest family in the neighbourhood, witnessing a complete change of age demographic in our area.

Our children had moved out and started their own families. Our house that was once full of activities, laughter and chaos is peaceful and quiet now. Indeed, a wheel of life. Back to basic just the two of us once again.

How long do we able to maintain our big house? How long can my husband be able to care for our back garden? Scary thoughts, but for now we just move on. We are so lucky that we are still healthy and enjoying the love and company of family and friends.

For how long will my husband and I will be able to celebrate together Christmas and New Year?.....My wish is to hopefully celebrate for another twenty more years or so!

Excerpt from
*Reflective Contemplations*

### ETERNAL FLAME

One of the sweetest things in life
Is to be able to share moments
With your loved ones up to the
Last journey of your life
To be able to look back together
Those beautiful and unforgettable memories
To be able to grow old together
Learning to accept each others
Faults and shortcomings
To be able to let the flame of love
We always cherish be
Forever in our hearts
Will remain as passionate as ever

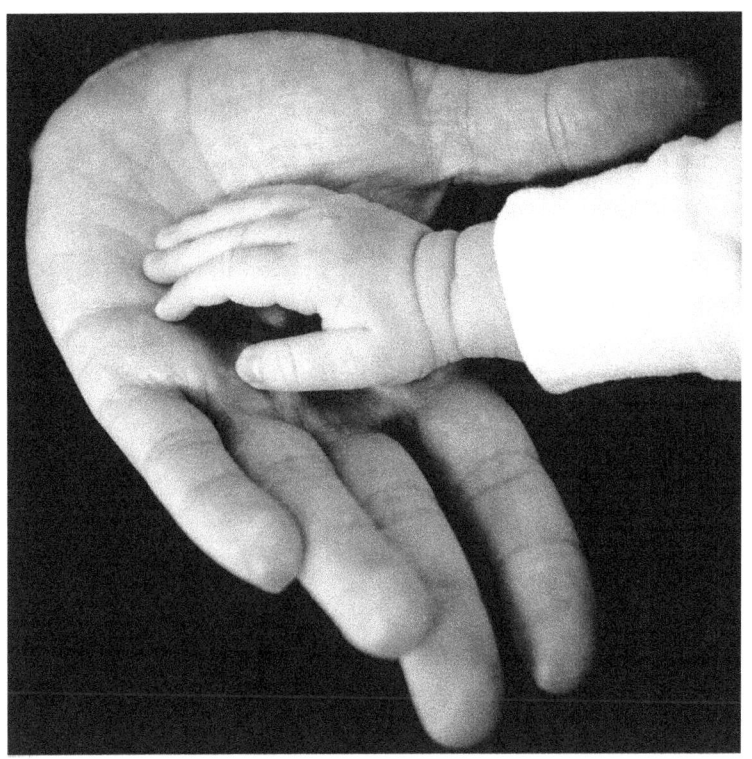

# 6
# A Christmas Story
# (True Story)

The Christmas season will always bring joy and happiness to all of us, and in the Philippines, it is one of the most celebrated events of the year. The Christmas of 1963 was the most memorable Christmas I'd ever had, and here is my story

In my younger days in the Philippines I was very active in our church and was the President of the Legion Of Mary at the Christ the King Church, Project 7 in Quezon city. This consisted of activities and duties such as catechism and leading block rosaries to name a few. One of the apostolic works that we did was visiting parishioners during weekends to spread the word of God and to support the elderly of our community.

While doing my apostolic work, I befriended an elderly lady by the name of Lola Rose. She was in her mid-eighties, with no family apart from her only son who was living in America with his wife and two sons. After Sunday's morning mass and church meeting, I always visited her. She would bake my favourite Chiffon and Cassava cakes.. We shared the same interests: in reading inspirational books and playing classical piano pieces. We talked about a lot of things , and every time she talked about her son and grandchildren , she would show a twinkle in her eyes.

Every December Lola Rose's son and his family come and visit her, and every Christmas eve I would visit her .and experience a great feeling of warmth to be a part of this beautiful family. On Christmas Eve she always cooked Pancit (noodle), Leche Plan (crème Caramel) Puto ( rice cake) and Dinuguan (pork blood stew) and of course a little gift wrapped with a beautiful ribbon as present for me.

One Sunday morning when I visited her she was crying, she said that her son won't be able to visit her this Christmas . Embracing her I assured her that she won't be lonely as my family will be there for her.

As promised I told my Dad on Christmas eve that I will be going early to visit Lola Rose , and then would head to the church afterwards in time for Christmas Eve Mass.. The door was open when I arrived at her house, but when I called her name there was no answer. I thought she must be asleep, so I let myself in. Passing through the kitchen I noticed she had already prepared the Leche Plan, Pancit puto and dinguan and a nice wrapped gift for me. Smiling I went to the bedroom, there was a note at the bedside saying " Dear Lorna, I am so tired I will have a small nap, please wake me up once you have arrived.

Lola was sleeping peacefully with a rosary on her hand, As I began to tenderly wake her up ,she was not responding to my voice and as I touched her, the body was cold as ice. I screamed and started sobbing in a confused panic ,my whole body ,trembling with shock

It will be more than five decades now since that harrowing experience but I will always remember with love the good old memories I shared with this lovely lady whom I fondly called as my Lola Rose.

Excerpt from
*My Innermost Thoughts*

Death will always leave
A gaping hole in our hearts
It will take time to heal
But, all the beautiful memories
Will always be Treasured

# 7
## Life Begins at "Any Age"

Contrary to a popular adage " Life Begins At Forty" I truly believe that Life Begins At Any Age. It was in the year 1932 that, an American Psychologist and writer Walter Pitkin, published a self help book which started the notion that Life begins at forty, hence pioneering the saying.

Every person is different . Depending upon the person's situational circumstance or even luck can play an important and major role in the lives of all of us. "Life Begins at Forty "is no longer relevant in today's environment. People live longer and are able to achieve and maximise their talents up to the twilight years of their lives.

There are people who are very successful at a very young age. Mark Zuckerberg launched his Face Book from his dormitory at the age of 20 on February 4,2004 making him a billionaire at a very young age. Other examples include singers and artists, one of them is Justin Bieber at the age of 16 became a household name and rose to stardom,

Sometimes success and fame overtake their young minds and souls, and they succumb to drugs and alcohols culminating to the end of their lives. Amy Winehouse, River Phoenix and many more talented artists, singers , are some whose lives were cut short because of the pressure of fame. However there are late bloomers, who discover and pursue their talents from their 70's and through their 90's.

At the age of 95, Nola Ochs from Jetmore Kansas graduated from the University in 2007 She was certified by the Guinness World Records as the oldest person to have a University degree. Grandma Moses, without basic training, started painting at the age of 75. And at the age of 101, one of her paintings was sold for $1.2 million dollars.

I started writing at age of 69, a talent that I did not know I had. Now I have published four books and a regular contributor of articles to the Philippine Times. Two years ago I decided to continue and pursue my passion for playing classical pieces, I enrolled in a Music School and next year I will be doing AMEB exam (Australian Music Examination Board) for grade eight intermediate level. This is prime time of my life definitely a late bloomer.

We should never stop learning, never stop doing exciting things and sometimes doing things out of our comfort zone, it is the spice of life We should continue to socialise and be active. Continue to be motivated and you will be surprised of what you can achieve. Suffice to say, the popular saying of Life begins at 40 is definitely obsolete in this modern technological era of TODAY!

Excerpt from
*My Innermost Thoughts*

Never stop learning
Never stop stimulating your brain
Never stop believing in yourself
Never stop following your dreams
Never stop doing things
You are passionate about
Continually Challenge yourself
After all life is too short
To be wasting your precious time.

# 8
# Spring of Life

Spring is my favourite season of the year Why? Because I believe Spring is full of surprises, excitements and adventures. It is a refreshing and enjoyable season to experience. The days become longer and the temperature becomes more pleasant.

My hither and thither plants and shrubs from the last Winter season are looking tidier since my husband started to spend more time in the garden. My roses Geranium and annuals are now in bloom, showcasing their magnificent flowers in rainbow colours, a feast for the eyes. A remarkable beauty of nature is to be experienced in Spring.

My Cherry, apple, Apricot, Plum, and Peach are all blossoming at their peak indicative of the abundance of fruits this coming Summer season. The fragrance smell of Jasmin flowers filled up my backyard garden especially during the night.

While doing my morning walk I can hear and see the birds coming back to the garden. Bees and butterflies are busy doing their jobs, sucking nectar from flower to flower. Spring is also the busiest season for the Honey- Bee and the Beekeeper

One of the many surprises of Spring are the deciduous plants , trees, shrubs which hibernate during Winter, and are now showing sign of life and growing stronger each day.

Why do we truly appreciate and welcome the Spring season? Because it is a stark contrast of the gloomy, dreary cold Winter season. Akin to our life's journey, the more adversities and struggles in life that we go through The more we appreciate the real essence of what happiness is all about. The more we can savour and value the joy of the sweet success in life.

Spring denotes life, hope and new beginning. So what are we waiting for? Spring into action and start doing things you put on hold. This is the time to pursue our goals and aspirations in life. Lets enjoy the Spring season as much as we can while it is here!

Excerpt from
*My Innermost Thoughts*

The season of Winter is akin to the darkest moments
Of our lives
Unforeseen traumatic tragedies will happen
As long as you have a solid faith in God
And the support of loved ones and friends
You can overcome all predicaments
Soon Spring will be around
New hope, new life and new beginning
Our journey will be rosier
And joyful than ever

# 9
# Worlds Apart

We all have our own journeys to the countries and destinations of our choosing. Whether it will be for business, holiday or balikbayan (overseas Filipino tourists), they will have memorable experiences and exciting adventures . My recent travel to Manila early this year was an unforgettable one that I would like to share to all.

With no immediate families such as parents and siblings in Manila, we stayed at a five star hotel in Makati. The hotel was a walking distance to SM, Glorietta, Greenbelt and Landmark(these are all shopping malls) As we entered the hotel I was overwhelmed by the luxury of the place. With Humongous foyer with magnificent chandelier, and the two grand stairways leading to spacious second floor foyer, It was such a lavish display of luxury. On the end of the first floor foyer, was a huge open space café lounge where a 14 piece band will entertain, playing contemporary, classical, jazz and modern music.

The following day my cousin picked us up in their car to go to SSS (Social Security System) Cavite to help me to get my SSS pension It took us only less than an hour for the approval of my pension, however we have to find a bank for my remittance , then the fun started. Leaving our car at the SSS , we walked along a footpath crowded with makeshift stores, full of half naked men staring at us. I felt uncomfortable with the situations. It was so hot, sunny and I was the only one wearing sunglasses. Hubby whisper and said do not wear your sun glasses . On the way to the bank we had to hop into a moving jeepney vehicle. Lucky my husband was there to help me in, as I I had forgotten to jump on. Finally we found a bank to deposit my SSS pension

Then again I had another traumatic experience when crossing the street. Being at the outskirt of Manila there were no traffic lights, you have to cross at your own risk. Although there were white lines on the road for crossing, cars and buses won't give way to pedestrians. I screamed and nearly died crossing the street, but I managed to pull through.

There was a very sharp contrast from some wealthy areas and tourist belt in the city. You can see so much poverty, but the people were happy, still smiling and friendly. Happiness is really subjective there are those people who got everything but have no peace within. Material things had overtaken their souls and spirit. This contrast was brought further to light when we returned to the hotel, where we were greeted by smiling gorgeous ladies who were eager to give you everything your heart desires but at a cost

I do love to visit the Philippines, its raw, vibrant, energetic and the people were so friendly. They were willing always to help you. Amidst the misery and poverty around, they were still smiling contented in their lives. People connect and bonded with one another. Even at night you can see people in groups outside their houses having fun sharing stories and laughing. In Australia you do not even know your neighbour's name. Is it because we are too busy in Australia working, or busy to gain earthly and worldly things that you do not have time to connect with people?

Will I be going back again? Of course I will . I love the food, the people and still love the Filipino values and culture.

Returning back in Australia I do appreciate more all the blessings we do enjoy here. Most of the times we had taken it for granted We are truly lucky to be in this beautiful adopted country of ours...
AUSTRALIA

*My unpublished inspirational message*

No matter what you do
No matter where you are
No matter what you are now
Whether you are successful or not
Do not forget your root
Where you came from

# 10
# Is it Fate or Destiny?

Did you ever question yourself for a phenomenon or a significant event that happened in your life? Did you wonder if it is fate or destiny?

Hitherto, these two words, fate and destiny are often misunderstood by a lot of people. The truth is they are entirely different in concept. Fate is something that can not be altered, no matter how hard we try. It is a pre-determined event that can happen without our choice and is beyond our control. Destiny is something that we have full control of, a choice and the desire to make it happen. Nonetheless, there are times that fate and destiny can go hand in hand. and can work effectively together.

You can not choose your parents, relatives nor the country of your birth. You can not choose also the timing of your death. These are only few of the many examples of fate. With destiny you can have a choice, explore your given talents, and chase your dreams and most of all a choice to be successful in life.

In a religious point of view, Christians believe that GOD has an intention and mission for us here on earth, but He also has given us free will to do the righteous way of living. IF we chose the wrong path, we should be responsible for our actions.

James 4:2 (NIV) " You desire but do not have, so you kill, you covet but you can not get, so you quarrel and fight. You do not have, but you do not ask God"

Indeed this is an ultimate example of our free will, and the choices we made will have a dire consequences in our lives. We also have a choice of connecting with God, but some continuously ignore that, and some have taken it for granted.

This is one of the many series of experiences of fate and destiny in my life. Most of you will remember the Port Arthur Massacre in Tasmania on the 28th of April 1996. My hubby and I had booked to visit on that very same date, but ..I had changed the date to one week before to 21st of April as I was informed that there would be festivities of Military parade, Police concert and lots of activities that will be happening. The Port Arthur massacre happened on the 28 of April 1996 Sunday at 1:00 at the Broad Arrow Café. The day and time that we were supposed to have our lunch as part of our tour itinerary. The Broad Arrow Café was quite small and the arrangement of tables were so closed together that it was easy for Martin Bryant to shoot people at the café.

I always have a shiver down my spine every time I remember this incident. It was my fate not to die yet, I believe I still have to fulfil a mission here on earth. At times there are occurrences that will happen in our lives that only God will know and have control of. Yes it is true we have a free will, a destiny to chase and follow but at the end it is the will of God that will prevail. The Lord's prayer venerated and prayed by billions of Christians around the world has this important message

"THY WILL BE DONE ON EARTH AS IT IS IN HEAVEN:

Excerpt from
*My Innermost Thoughts*

Realities of Life
Each time we breathe to live
Each time we should remember that life is a gamble
Each time is a challenge
Each time is a journey because no one knows
What the future brings and holds
Yes we can try to plan and control our lives
But much to our dismay we soon discover
We can only do it to a certain degree
So as not to be bitterly disappointed, accept the things
You can not change
If you can change things, do them better next time
Indeed these are the REALITIES OF LIFE

# 11
## For the Love of God

FATHER FORGIVE THEM, FOR THEY KNOW NOT WHAT THEY ARE DOING. Luke 23:34. Today you will be with me in paradise, Luke 23:43. These were the first and second last words of Christ on the cross. Christ humbled himself accepting the will of God to die for our sins. These are the real substance of the meaning of Lent, that is to practice humility and forgiveness as manifested by our lord Jesus Christ.

Lent is the most important celebration and commemoration of the death of Christ on the cross by all Christians around the world. Lent is the 40 days celebrations before Easter ( the time of the resurrection of Christ) This is the time for reflections, fasting, repentance, spiritual discipline and most of all forgiveness and humility. After Lenten season, there will be Easter family celebrations, Easter egg hunting, lots of chocolates and sweets. Joyous celebrations for Christ resurrection. For non -believers this is a time for holidays and time off from work. Nonetheless for Christians , no matter how earnest and intense your prayers are, if your heart is full of hate, greed or envy, the sacred time is meaningless.

During the Lenten season countries from different congregation will have their own ways of celebrating. Generally, they make small sacrifices such as giving up certain things they enjoy doing. Some people fast and abstain from eating meat during Lenten Fridays. In the Philippines even though the Catholic church disapproves of performing the penitence , there are people whipping themselves on their backs with bundles of bamboo sticks tied to a length of rope . until their backs will be covered with blood. People are still doing this for repentance of sins.

The Lenten season is also a reminder to all of us that amidst all the suffering and conflict we are going through, there will always be a glimmer of hope, akin to the celebration of Easter, the resurrection of Christ.

According to Matthew 7:23 Christ said " Not everyone who said LORD, LORD will enter the kingdom of heaven, but the one who does the will of my Father WHO is in heaven. "In the realm of religion and Christianity we are encourage to go to church every Sunday to pray and give homage to GOD. However, there are those who pray often and regularly , yet their hearts are as cold as ice and full of deceit . Will they have a place in Heaven? In contrast There are agnostic, atheist people but their hearts are pure, kind and caring, Will these people have a place in heaven. Indeed these are two extreme examples, but I firmly believe that your actions, the way you treat people , and if you have an inner peace within yourself and others , is what really matter

Excerpt from
*My Innermost Thoughts*

Prayers are not the only way to communicate with God
There are other ways, such as a simple act of kindness to others
I am close to mother nature while working in my garden
I can show my appreciation of all the beautiful creations
He had given us
I am a good mother, grandmother, friend and respect for others
Following all HIS commandments and what matters
most is following
All that HE preaches. These are more potent ways
Of expressing my love for "HIM" other than prayers!!

## 12
## The Most Beautiful Face on Earth

A little boy was crying, looking for his mother. A stranger came and ask the little boy, "where is your mum and can you describe what does she look like?" which the little boy replied" My mum has the most beautiful face on earth" The stranger, in search for a beautiful lady and said to the boy, " Is this your mum ?" the boy said ' No my mum is prettier than her. A few times the stranger tried to bring beautiful ladies and each time the boy said that his mum is prettier. Then a plain looking lady came and said " There you are I had been looking for you !" The little boy's face brightened with gladness and proudly said to the stranger, " You see my mum has the most beautiful face on earth"

Indeed , through the eyes of children their mothers are the most beautiful for them, true to the saying that BEAUTY IS IN THE EYES OF THE BEHOLDER.

A face that only a mother can love is another expression we say about the unconditional love a mother can offer to her children. From the moment of conception, followed by birth and the first taste of milk of a baby from their mother's bosom , There is an immeasurable bonding between a mother and her child.

While the children are growing up they will feel and vision their mothers as a protector, who gives them love and kindness and showers them with lots of hugs and kisses . Thus in their minds without any doubt their mother will be the most wonderful and beautiful person on earth..

Those sleepless nights, sacrifices made especially for working mums, a mother will endure to nurture and care for their children. A mother is a teacher, disciplinarian, provider, protector, mediator rolled in to one. No job can outdo what mother can do and I believe being a mother is the most noble, challenging, and difficult job, but its all worth it !!!.

Mothers have a big influence in shaping the character of their children. A responsible mother will produce responsible adults because mothers serve as a role model for their children. This is a precious gift all mothers can offer to the society and the wider community.

It is fleeting to say just for that special day of every 2nd Sunday of May, we should all toast to celebrate and ,recognise the significant role of all mothers in the world. However our appreciation for them should always be given at all times…………..

HAPPY MOTHER'S
DAY TO ALL THE BEAUTIFUL MOTHERS
AROUND THE WORLD!!

Excerpt from
*My Passion My Calling*

## MOTHERS

It is in the mother's heart
That children can find
Assurance of being loved
It is in the mother's arms
That the children can find
Solace and comfort
BUT
It is in the mother's hugs and kisses
That the children can find the real joy

# 13
## Thanks for the Memories

Each year will come and go, so will be this year. At the end of each year we are always in the process of preparing, assessing and evaluating the things we had done and had happened in our lives. There are memories that can be forgotten but there are some that can linger on forever and will always makes us happy.

Both pleasant and painful memories can happen for the past year, and for the unfortunate ones, this is the time to move on and try to embrace the coming new year with hope, new life and a new beginning. From the past mistakes we can now set up new goals and aspirations. For grieving families who lost loved ones, remember to concentrate for the living loved ones who still need your care and support.

It is no use having a long list of New Year's resolution. Based from statistic only 8% people will keep their New Year's resolution. Nonetheless remember that the choices we made will create and shape our future.

Be practical and sensible when making a resolution, start with the easiest one, take baby step and when you feel you are ready you can set or aim for your next goal. By doing this it won't create disappointment and frustrations.

Prioritise what is important, but consider as well that your changes will benefit not only yourself but your loved ones. Ask you family for support if needed and I am sure they will always be there for you.

I am truly thankful for the memories for the year 2017. It was the year that we celebrated our 50th wedding anniversary, the same year I had launched my 3rd book and my first novel "Moments of Love, Lust and Ecstasy. The previous year I decided to continue my piano study and fortunate enough to pass the Australian Music Examination Board for intermediate level (AMEB).

This time I won't be making any New Year's Resolution instead I will continue my passion for writing, music and supporting my Charities, most especially The National Breast Cancer Foundation.

Thanks for the outgoing year 2017 for all the wonderful memories I have and I hope next year ahead in 2018 will be the same or even better for me and for all of us.

Excerpt from<br>
*My Innermost Thoughts*

Excerpt from my book<br>
*It is the choice we make in our lives*<br>
*That makes life itself*<br>
*Full of challenges and surprises*<br>
*Hence shaping and creating*<br>
*Our journey of life*

# 14
# The Many Faces of Happiness

> Happy are those who can forgive
> Because they will find peace
> Within themselves and others
> Happy are those who stay connected with God
> Because it is the only way to eternal salvation
> Happy are those who are willing to share and help others
> Because they make a difference in this troubled world we live in
> And lastly happy are those who can love and accept people
> Because they will be loved in return
>
> **By Lorna Ramirez**

Happiness will truly define who, what we are and what our priorities are in life. We go through different stages of happiness as we walk the journey of life. A small child will find happiness by playing with pots and pans or even by pulling tissues from a tissue box, ignoring expensive toys given by dotting parents. Expression of delight and joy on children's' faces when surrounded with candies, chocolates, cakes, and ice cream; those are simple gestures of happiness through the eyes of children.

As we grow older happiness becomes complicated. We set goals, achievements, and power. An ultimate happiness by many of us. For some people, there are those whose happiness can be achieved by sharing and helping others such as missionaries, community workers, soldiers, to name a few. They are special people who have talents that an "Almighty God" has provided them to share.

At the middle of our journey in life a different level of happiness is felt when we meet our soulmate or the love of our life, then becoming a parent. Sheer joy of happiness is experienced when we had our first born child. Our children are an extended version of ourselves, nurture them with love and they will do the same once they have families of their own. No greater happiness can be felt by parents knowing that their children lead a happy and successful life.

My own experience of happiness was that moment where I had the chance to hold my first born granddaughter. From the very first time that I laid eyes on her, I knew that I was blessed to be her grandmother. As I walk through life nearing the end of my journey, my happiness consists of looking after my grandchildren, being there for their first smile, first uttered words, and their first steps. It is an exuberant experience to be a grandmother, and I believe that all grandparents can relate to this.

As a guest speaker at one of the events that I attended I could feel the frustration and loneliness of the elderly. They felt left out and seeking for the attention, love, and care of their families. Fortunately in Australia, we have elderly organisations that are doing a fantastic job to help and entertain them with various activities that can alleviate their loneliness.

At the end we must remember that we will all grow old, and

when the time comes it's up to us to make our own lives interesting regardless of your age.

Akin to the happiness of a child, as we walk through the final journey our happiness becomes simple and uncomplicated. Indeed this is the cycle of life. As we grow older we also realise that *the simplest things in life are often the best.*

# 15
# Chrysalis My Journey as an Author

(Excerpt from my book My Passion My Calling)

Every Sunday morning as often as possible, we attended mass in our community Parish church. Today's Sunday was no different. It was bright sunny day, Chris and I decided to take a walk after mass in the nearby Tea Garden Park opposite our house. We hurriedly went home and changed to our walking gear.

I do love walking with Chris, admiring those majestic trees along the river banks of the Maribyrnong river. And also feasting my eyes with the natural rock formations of different shapes and colours.

The Tea Garden is complete with barbecue facilities and I playground ideal for families get together. Remember Chris? When our children were young they loved this place. Yes I know how time flies now it is just the two of us. Chris said with a sadness in his voice. Be happy Chris you have two beautiful grandchildren and you still have me, I replied.

Feeling tired after walking for few hours I said " Chris I am tired I've had enough. Let's start walking home. Chris agreed " okay we will head home and rest

It was almost noon so I prepared our lunch then rested and

watched TV. Suddenly I felt an intense pain at the back of my abdomen spreading to my groin and leg. I am with pain and scream; Chris help I need help ! Chris rushed from the bedroom into the family room. Evelyn what's wrong honey I will call triple 000

My face was pale then I felt blood coming from my behind. I was bleeding heavily. Ambulance came and drove me to Western General Hospital. I was given a blood transfusion ,subjected to a CT scan that found out I had an abdominal aneurysm. I undergone a procedure called Aneurysm Embolisation, a risky procedure that can damaged the bowel and surrounding vessels.

After more than three hours of surgery I felt coldness beginning at my feet, envelop my whole body. It seemed as though the world stood still and that I had travelled through time. Serenity, complete peace, calmness. ...I experienced all of these. Then I saw rows of flowers, their fragrances greeting my senses. My whole body was feeling light as if I was walking in clouds. My surroundings were all in white.

At the far end I could visualise a tunnel and at the end of the tunnel a striking glittering brightness that almost blinded my eyes. I would have liked to have gone inside but my mind was saying no. Slowly I walked to the tunnel but at the moment I tried to step inside the door shut.

Then I woke up and heard the nurse saying " Mrs Valdez stay with us open your eyes. She kept doing a tender slap on my face. She said urgently " Doc, the blood pressure is at dangerous level even the heart beat and pulse are low" The Doc said" Only a few seconds more I think I have done it well. Lets hope no complications will happen. The procedure lasted almost four hours ,I had used so many litres of blood that it seemed that my entire blood must have been replenished. Then they moved me to a recovery room. The following day the surgeon visited me in my room and said" I am happy with the outcome. According to the scan the coil was successfully placed at the ruptured blood vessel. I did not tell my family what had happened at the theatre

Months passed I was doing well, full of energy and back to my routine. It was Father's Day, all my family was at my place. I was busy cooking ,but I always treasured the special moments to be with loved ones. At this time I asked Michelle my daughter to sign me up on face book. She laughed and said" Mum you hate writing and besides Face Book is only for young ones. With my persistence she obliged. I surprised myself I could write. I didn't know where my thoughts and ideas were coming from. Each time I was at the computer I started writing poems, inspirational messages and quotes, all base on my strong beliefs and convictions. Never in my wildest dreams did I imagine I would be able to do it.

Chris could see the change in me and one day at the breakfast table he asked" Evelyn what's got in to you? You started having interest in writing, which I know you always hated I have not heard you play for decades, but now you started tickling the ivory keys.. What has happened? I Replied I do not have any explanation Chris, I just feel my passion for writing and music in my heart. He responded" I think there is something that has happened to trigger you enthusiasm. I said" I can not think of anything else except that I was hospitalised for abdominal aneurysm. Chris laughed and said 'HA HA HA you believe that, you and your imagination.

For almost one and a half years I kept on writing until one afternoon another ordeal in my life happened. Chris was beside me at our kitchen bench table while I was sorting out oye groceries, suddenly I had double vision, passed out for few seconds. I found myself in the arms of Chris, preventing me from falling and hitting my head on the floor. Ambulance was called and I was rushed to the Western General Hospital. The MRI confirmed that I had a congenital brain aneurysm. It was only small so it was inoperable. I was given a blood thinning tablet and with healthy diet ,it will be controlled.

After this frightening episode, I decided to write a book to have a legacy for my family, friends and relations. I started organising and accumulating all my writings from Facebook and my notes and scribbles. I found it daunting organising everything . It took me few weeks to accomplish it. My manuscript was sent to many publishers. Being an unknown author I found it difficult. Several publishers rejected my work. Feeling disappointed and frustrated, I turned to my husband and said " Chris I don't think I will have a chance to pursue my dream. Chris said" Don't stop following your dream . Keep on trying, I know you will be able to make it.. This is typical of Chris, my very supportive husband, who was always giving hope and encouragement about what I was doing.

Browsing through the internet, I came across a publishing company, I rang them and they agreed to have a look at my manuscript. It was a nervous wait. Two weeks passed, feeling nervous but hopeful, I received an email from the publisher. The editor loved my manuscript and recommended for publication I jumped with joy, ran to Chris who was busy at the backyard, hugged him and screamed at the top of my voice 'Chris at last I will be an author. Chris said " I am overjoyed and very happy for you Evelyn, I 've had faith always in you. I always knew you can do it.

Finally I received the first copy of the book, impressed with the book I ordered two hundred copies. The whole family was excited especially my granddaughter Kaitlin who said" Wow Grandma this is the first time my name is in the book. I said "Of course, sweetie. This will not be the last time more will be coming. Then her eyes brightened and she gave me a hug

I then organised two book launches at my place. All the family were involved in presentation and arrangement. My son -in law Edward suggested that I should have a launch in Bendigo, saying quite a few people would be interested in buying the book. The following month in the last month of August my book was launched at Bendigo .My son in-law's family and friends and all of my families were there to support me. I was excited and quite nervous but it turned out to be a success. One of the Edward's family friend invited me for a afternoon tea, Of course I said yes. My children and their partners headed home, Simone and Kaitlin stayed with us.

Edward's friend's place was beautiful, Emma and her husband George were lovely couple and very friendly. Rows of beautiful geranium, roses and begonias of different colours were planted in the front yard, mixed with native shrubs and trees. They had a big veranda at the back of the house where we have our tea, biscuits and cakes.

The children Kaitlin and Simone were playing football in the spacious backyard full of fruit trees, a veggie patch and again rows of beautiful roses and geraniums. Even the Veranda was filled with hanging begonias of different colours. Chris and George were busy tackling politics, and other topics. As I entered the veranda I felt something ---as if I knew the place. Sitting at the veranda having a cup of tea , Emma said " I wish my daughter Tessa was here. I said where is Tessa now? Tears started to fill Emma's eyes. She's gone four years ago in a car accident 16th of May 2010 at 4:00 pm

I experienced goose bumps ,cold shivers and shock I could hardly breathe — that day I will always remember. May 16, 2010 at 4:00 pm was when I had a near death experience during my abdominal surgery. Emma said " What's wrong Mrs Valdez? You feeling okay you looked pale, want a glass of water? I am okay no problem Thanks. Emma continued " Tessa loved poetry and always dreamed one day of having her book published.

She was also a good classical pianist. We really miss her. I will show you her room still untouched exactly as it was before she died. I will also show you all her writings. They are almost identical as yours. Please come inside.

I followed Emma inside. Again I had a feeling of familiarity with the place as if I had been here all my life. Her room "Tessa" was at the far end , the first room near the front door. We entered the bedroom: again the smell, the sights were so close to my senses and heart. Familiarity reigned once more.

Emma handed me a neatly kept file of writings inside an envelope. Upon reading Tessa's writings I realised that although different words were used, the meanings, themes. Messages were almost identical to mine.

I heard Chris's voice at the veranda saying "C'mon Evelyn we have to keep moving. The grandchildren have to be dropped off at their place.. I replied ' Okay Chris". I kissed and hugged Emma and George. Such a lovely couple to lose their only child. I did not say anything about the connection between Tessa and me.

Emma said "It was strange but I could feel I had a good connection with you the moment I saw you. I said "Same with me Emma. Really nice meeting both of you and for sure this will not be our last time. Hope we will be seeing each other some time. Emma replied "Of course you can visit us anytime and you can bring your grand children. They are so adorable.

Driving home that afternoon, I was quiet, Chris looked at me and said" Evelyn you have not said a word since we left. Anything bothering you? I Replied "Its okay I just feel exhausted after a long day. Nothing to worry about. But in my mind I know the reason why I was still here……..To continue the mission and calling. One day I will explain to Chris and to the beautiful couple Emma and George. That will be ……..when the time is right.

There are some things in our lives  
We can not comprehend or explain  
Beautiful moment can always happen  
Always Chase your DREAMS and your DESTINY  
BY Lorna Ramirez

# Inspirational Messages and Thoughts

There is nothing more stronger and admirable than the hearts
who care, share and understand

No one is too old to continue chasing their passions.
Just focus and persevere till you
Reach your goal.

Truly I can say there are friends who are worth keeping
And those you can live without
Treasure those who are!

We laughed, we cried
We loved, we grieved
Have you learned something from these?

What is the secret of a successful person?
They always remain humble
And they don't forget their root and the people
Who helped them

# Chasing My Passion and My Calling

LORNA RAMIREZ

First published in Australia 2015
This edition published 2018
Copyright © Lorna Ramirez 2015
Cover design, typesetting: Working Type Studio, Melbourne

The right of Lorna Ramirez to be identified as the Author of the Work has been asserted in accordance with the Copyright, Designs and Patents Act 1988.

All rights reserved. No part of this publication may be reproduced, stored in a retrieval system, or transmitted, in any form or by any means without the prior written permission of the publisher, nor be otherwise circulated in any form of binding or cover other than that in which it is published and without a similar condition being imposed on the subsequent purchaser.

Ramirez, Lorna
*Chasing my Passion and My Calling*
ISBN (pbk): 978-0-6482130-4-8
ISBN (ebook): 978-0-6482130-5-5
pp118

Sources of Information:

Footscray Historical Society

Heritage Place Victoria, Heritage Overlay no. HO135, Hermes number 35583, File Number PL-HE/03/0929

Expectations will always lead
To heartaches and disappointments
Its nice to be surprised

Although the passing years had taken away
Our youthful and physical beauty, but through
The years it strengthen our souls and changed
Our perspective in life

It is in what we believe
That makes us strong
It is in whom we love
That inspires us

I had done my legacy
And fully satisfied with my life
Regardless of whatever happens

With every breath I take
With every sigh I made, the thought of you
Will forever embedded in my heart

It is in the mother's love
We can realised what loving
Is all about

There are some moments
In your life worth reminiscing
And will always have
Special place in your heart

Sometimes negativity from others
Will inspire you to achieve
Your utmost goal
And proven them wrong

Life is such a big lottery
You do not have a choice
Coming here on earth

Life will be empty
Without love, dreams, and convictions

In love we can rediscover
Our inner self
And our hidden strength

There are times in your life
A certain event that happened
Will entirely change
Your perspective in life

Chasing your dream is one thing
Taking action is another story

Running away for things that matter
Will only lead to disappointments

True love will always
Find the way

Declutter your heart with unimportant things
To let "HIM" reign in your heart

Fame and success will not guarantee
The "Holy Grail" of happiness
And peace within

Whenever you are at your lowest ebb
Just think of all your blessings
Your smile will be back

Life is not always a bed of roses
Learn to deal with good and bad ones
Many things we can encounter
As we walk the journey of our lives

It is not the quantity
But the quality of friends
That matter most

Be not deceived by smiling faces
At times their hearts
Are as cold as Ice

If you are constantly blaming others
And not accepting responsibilities for your actions
You will never find the reason
For your existence here on earth

Sometimes choosing which passion to follow
Is akin to choosing who is your favourite child

It really feels good if you do not expect
Anything and if the outcome is surreal
Happiness

Realities of life…At times
New friends are the ones who
Will support you and your advocacy

To have a strong belief will
Inspire a person to follow
Their passions. Dreams and goals in life

It is so easy for us to see the faults of others
But blinded to see our own inadequacies
Its easy for us to judge others

But we react negatively, when being judge
It's easy for us to point the mistake of others
But defensive when it is our mistakes
Though no one is perfect
Being aware of all your shortcomings
Is vital for improvement , hence you can be
A better person than you are now

Start with a dream
Then the imaginary concept
Becomes a Reality
The result will be an ultimate HAPPINESS

I believe a person is considered Rich
Not by material wealth
And not by what he has
But by what he is

Regardless of whatever be the situations
Always be yourself
And it will work out for the best

Traumatizing moments are only temporary
What matters most
Are lessons learned from these

Material things will come and go
But the purity, honest and kindness

Of your spiritual soul
Will always be remembered

Transform your heartaches, failures and disappointments
Into one whole -learning experience and wisdom
For one's self and others

Do not crucify yourself by doing things
Just because people are expecting you to do
Do the things you enjoy and love doing
This way you are making the favour for yourself

There are those who lived their whole lives
Without finding love
Lucky are those even though
Their lives are cut short
They had experienced
How it is to love and be loved.

Your priority in life
And what matters to you
Will truly define
Who you are

Without sorrow and pain
We won't know the real meaning of happiness
Without love there is no joy of living
Without faith and hope

We won't have any strength and inspiration
Most importantly
Without our strong connection with GOD
We will find it hard to go
Through the hard times and trial in our lives

True love lingers on
Up to the last breath of our lives
Sacrifices will turn to glory
For the one you love and adore

The magical power of a camera
Capturing that beautiful second
Of motion and moment, that only
A click of the camera can do
This can not be retrieved nor repeated

The realization of my dream
Is my Holy Grail

If your heart is filled with love
And care, giving and sharing
Will always be easy

Pretence and hypocrisy will never last
At the end you can no longer
Hide behind the mask
Truth will prevail

There are things that we cannot bring back
What had been taken from us
Enjoy what was left
To bring closure
To our lives

In times of sorrow
We prayed and remember Him
In times of abundance
Do we still remember Him?

Rejection, disappointments are sometimes
Can make you stronger
More determined than ever
To do things you are passionate about
These are the catalysts that can
Drive you to success, to seek perfection
Until you can achieve all the goals
You are aiming for

We try so hard deceiving others
But at the end we get confused
Who we really are

It is in what we believe
That will shape
Our Present and future life

A life full of love
Is life full of bliss


The most beautiful things in life
That can not be touch nor seen
Is called LOVE


All of us have gone through several stages in life
Each stage is a learning experience
At the end it is nice to look back
Not counting the years you have gone through
But counting the special moments
That you had been through


It does not matter what they say
It does not matter what they think of you
It does not matter how they judge you
What matters most is being happy
Happy for the things you do
And believing in yourself

The past will have a big impact
Of what we are now
Others will move on
But there are those who will be ruined
And scarred for life


Life is so simple
Why do we have to make it so complicated?
Aftermath of modern civilization


It is who I am that matters
And not what you want me to be


It is not about making it to the top
Being successful and famous in your career
It is all about giving back
Generously to the community
Some of your time
Specially to those needing the most

Letting it go does not mean forgetting the past
It is merely a preparation
For the new beginning
New life, new hope
Use your past as an inspiration
For a better future


Amidst your frustrations and disappointments
These will help you re-evaluate
Your priorities in life
What is important and what is not


Do not underestimate the power of words
The power of writing
It can do more harm than you ever realise
It can destroy a person's reputation


We should always know our own limitations
The time to stop and re-assess your priority
At times we are so immersed in our fame and success
That we think we are indestructible
Soon it is too late to know that we are not

Words are more lethal and fatal weapon
At times it go straight to your heart
And the pain is so excruciating


It is your choice, your decision
To make your life fruitful or a failure
Happiest moments in my life
Is when surrounded by my loved ones

## THE PURSUIT OF HAPPINESS

Waking up each day without
Expecting anything
Always thanking each day
For my blessings I have
Savouring each moment
What life has to offer
Enjoying the fullest
The beautiful surroundings
Beautiful people such as
Loved ones and friends
Whom they had given me joy
And making my journey of life
Interesting and meaningful
And most importantly
Had a part of making me
What I am today

At times we falter and failed
But that is not important
What matters most
Is how quickly we stand up
And do it all over again
This time we had learned your lesson
And we are more prepared than ever
And more determined to succeed
The second time around

Others hide their sorrows through their smiles
Others hide their fears by acting fearlessly
Others hide their insecurity by being boastful all the time
Others hide their inferiority by
acting superior to everyone
At times things that we see are not really what they are
There are more depths and meanings to consider
BEFORE JUDGING

**MY FAITH**
With every quest I had gone through
With every trial I had endured
With every frustration I had suffered
With every fall I had
Without a doubt in my mind
I will be able to overcome all these
Because I know these trying times
God will guide and lead me
To find the right path to cross

Trust should be balanced
Too trusting
You will find yourself
Taken advantage
While not trusting anyone
At times can be a miss opportunity

True character of a person
Will be revealed
If intoxicated frustrated and angry

Love is always forgiving, understanding and caring

Just like respect, trust
Should be earned
And not be given freely

Have you ever wonder and be bewildered
By the beauty and fragrance of the rose?
Amidst the thorns, that can symbolise our sufferings
Our trials and tribulations
Once conquered at the end is
The beautiful glorious beauty of a Rose
That symbolise our achievement

It is in what we believe
That will shape our present
And future life

I wish I could be remembered
Not by who I was
But what I was
And the things I did
During my living years

At times we can learn
Something
From the innocence, purity
And unadulterated mind
Of a child

There are moments that the
Sweetest words to be heard
Are those that are yet unspoken
And still buried in one's heart

It is not the quantity of friends
But the quality of friends matter

The safest place to be
Is in someone's heart and mind
Who will always love and care for you
And will always be there for you
Regardless

Everything done in excess
Becomes a poison
Irrespective of what they are

The worst regret in my life
Is not doing enough
What my heart desires
Not knowing of the possible results

A person who always lies
At the end will not know
The difference
Between the truth and the lies

Our conscience is responsible
For making us of what we are today
It helps shapes our beliefs, convictions
And our character. However there are times
It can be overtaken by greed such as power, fame and money
Let us hope we can be aware
Of these temptations

Life is full of surprises and regardless
Of what they are we should always
Be prepared and flexible
And be able to cope everything
That cross our path
Lucky are those who have support
From families and friends
But think of those
Who got no one to turn to

We do not expect to live forever
So make each day a celebration of life
Each day thanking him for
All the graces we have
Savour each precious moment
You spend with loved ones, families and friends
If you fail to do so
You will miss the most important
Things in your life
That money could not buy

It is in the realm of one's experience
That we learn to know
What is right or wrong
What is ethical or not
But some are just too stubborn
To accept their past mistakes
Relentlessly doing the same mistakes
Over and over again

There are moments
That are precious
That we tend to relive and remember
Each time. It makes us happy and puts
A smile on our faces
But there are memories that should be
Forgotten and instead serve as a lesson
Learned in our lives

Sometimes what we had seen and perceived
Are not really what they are. Because often times
Evil can mask in the shadow of goodness

An act of kindness
Done whole heartedly
One should not expect
Anything in return

In the midst of darkness
Love will always find its way
And brightens your path

There are those people who
Are getting their satisfaction by acting aggressively
To free themselves from the wrong deeds they had done
A subtle way of self-gratification

Such a beautiful gesture of friendship
When they are always there
To help you in time of needs
Support you in time of sorrow
Guide and lead you
When you are confused, and lost
For sure they are worth more than gold

Victory will be joyful and glorious
After each peril we had gone through

Without your faith and guidance
From God, you will be lost
Like a child wandering in the forest
With nowhere to go
And through "Him" you will see
The light and the way

Do not just follow the flow
Scrutinise, analyse
And it will lead you
To the right path

Greed, megalomaniac
Are akin to cancer
Slowly creeping and destroying
Your soul

One should always be wary
If you are only being used
For their own personal interest

A kind- hearted person
Will always see the goodness
Of others

Hurting and demeaning a person
Is not an option
And should always be avoided

The worst part of human behaviour
Is stepping someone's toes
Just to achieve their goals

We are so conscious
About the issue of political correctness
That refrain us from voicing our opinion

Loving someone has its negative side
You feel the pain when you see them hurting
You worry and pray that nothing will happen to them
You wish and hope that they will be able to cope up
With the challenges along the way
In spite of these I will say
These are only a small price to pay
For the blessings, blissful happiness
And joy of having someone to love
And in return to be loved.

Precious friends will become
Strangers due to unforeseen circumstance

I am meek as a lamb
But once Threaten and taken advantage of
I will be as ferocious as a lion

Greed, hungry for power, divide a nation
Destroyed friendship
Split families…… Harsh realities of life

Doesn't matter how and what they think of you
What matters is following your conscience
Following the truth

I believe that the main question about life
Is not all about yourself
But its all about what you had done
To help others, love others as you love yourself
To use your talents not only for yourself
But also for the benefit of mankind

Anything fighting
For a cause
Is worthwhile
Regardless of the aftermath

In times of trouble
You will know and realised
Who are your genuine friends

Amidst the turmoil and pain
Have faith in "Thee"
Solutions will be on your way

We tried as much as we can to hold on something
No matter how precious it was
There will come a time
We have to let it go
And continue to move on

You won't be able to see
What lies beneath
The mountain
Till you have the courage to climb it

Evil is around and within us
If you let it conquer you
It will destroy your body, spirit and soul

Happy are those who can forgive
Because they can easily attain
Inner peace within themselves
And fellowman

Reliving the moments
Of once beautiful memories
Can always bring
Sunshine and hope
Especially when one
Is in the middle
Of a personal conflict

Though we are human
We still have the power to choose
To be evil and righteous
To be a success or a failure
To be miserable and happy
To be moral and indecent
To be just or unjust
To be truthful or deceitful
Whatever you choose
Will determine
Who and what you will be
Now and the future
You should be responsible for your life
And no one else


Perhaps the most agonising
Pain of all
Is the one still deep in your heart
That no one can see or tell
But you are the only one
Who can feel and bear


Don't let your generosity
Be against you
At times people can
Manipulate and abuse you
For their own benefit

And satisfaction
Mother
When no one can understand me
My mother will
When no one loves me
My mother will
With all her heart
When I am all alone and in sorrow
My mother will
Comfort me
When I am confused and no where to go
My mother will
Guide and lead me
No one can have such a kind of love
Such a deep and intense love of a mother

It is up for us to live our life
To the fullest
Age is not a barrier
To do things
You are passionate about
There will always be a room
For improvement
Discovering your self
And never stop
Your quest for knowledge

## TO ALL MOTHERS

Each gift of the breath of life
A mother plays a crucial part
Suffice to say
It is indeed deserving
To celebrate the most important
Person on earth

## MOTHERS

They are so forgiving, and understanding
They will always be there for you
Regardless of all circumstances
Knows the real essence
Of what sacrifices is all about
A wonderful loved person by all

## GIFT TO MANKIND
## EXCERPT FROM MY BOOK
*My Innermost Thoughts*

It is with giving that we find the joy of sharing
It is in loving that we can fully feel how it is to be loved
It is in understanding that we can practise the art of compassion
It is in believing in ourselves that we can focus and do
Anything our heart desire
And most importantly
It is in trusting and believing in him
That we can find all the inspiration and courage to do these things

Giving does not mean expecting
To receive in return
Loving does not mean
Changing the person
For your own self intent
Believing does not mean
Being blinded and shielded
From facing the truth
Hoping does not mean
Not realising
Your own limitations and inadequacies

Always be wary because at times
You will see is only an illusion
And can be deceiving

To invest in education
Is the most noble charity
You can give to all
Especially those needing the most

At times to be hurt is needed"
To evaluate your past
Present and your future

The difference between a successful person
And a loser
The first will see opportunity around them
While the later will see negativity and often will give up
Even before trying

EXCERPT FROM MY BOOK
REFLECTIVE CONTEMPLATIONS

**SIMPLE LESSONS IN LIFE**
It is always best to have moments of evaluation
Assessment and recollection of the
Things happening in your life
You should make priorities of what is important
Be with people who care, love and support you
Who will be there for you
Regardless of the situation
Disconnect to those
Who don't appreciate you
Do not be affected with criticism
Instead us the criticism for your own advantage
Hence making you a better and stronger person

Any "life changing experience"
Will always make us re-assess
And evaluate our lives
There are times what was important before
Will be no longer relevant at present
You tend more to focus to the important
Things in life such as your families and friends
And less of the material things

Some people will criticise you
For what they don't have
And abhor you for your success
An ugly side of human nature

Loving and living the life you live is one thing
But loving and living your life with dignity
Honour , and stay connected with "HIM"
Are things we should aspire
And that is what matter most

Count your blessings first
Before complaining
All your miseries and frustrations
The first one will help you realise
How lucky you are than others

You cannot put a good person down
No matter how much you tried
They will survive and excel at the end

There are memories
That are too precious to be forgotten
Especially our childhood memories
They will always bring a smile to our face
Moments deeply treasured in our hearts

Everything changes
People, places, things surrounding us
We also change through the years
Physically, emotionally, and spiritually
Loving someone means continually
Accepting them for what they are today
Rather than they were yesterday

It is in what we believe and our convictions
That make us who and what we are today
It is what we fight for that
Makes us stronger than ever
And most of all
It is our love and compassion
That can easily open our hearts
So we can help the people who need the most

Those who suffered abuse
Had pain and disappointments in life
Will emerge either as
Stronger souls
Or a person full of hatred of vengeance
At the end
Becoming the abusers
Aggressors themselves

There are times
We want to leave
Away from the past
But the past never leaves us
Keeps on haunting us
Wherever and whenever we are
And it is up to us to accept
And deal with it courageously

Regardless of what had happened
Regardless of what reasons they are
One must face life with courage
Continue to move on
Just for the sake of all the people
Who still love and care for you

Always be happy and do not worry
Too much of what others will say
Follow your heart
Avoid negativity
Think positive
And you will get
Positive result

Good services to humanity
Will follow, after you forget
All your worldly desire of fame
Greed and fortune

Recipe for success
Be yourself
Stay simple
Be humble
No one wants a person
Too big for their shoes

As long as you are aware and believe
That you are in the right path
That you are making the right decision
Following what your hear dictates
Don't listen to what others will say
Be strong and firm, follow your instinct
And success is within your reach

Make each day a celebration
Of life
A life full of hope
A life full of positive attitude
Negativity will always
Produce stress and unhealthy
For the mind spirit and soul

Love is a universal language
Love encompasses everything
Defies reasons, logic and conquers
All along its path
No one can be immune to
Its power regardless of who you are

Excerpts from my book
*My innermost Thoughts*
Each time we breathe to live
Each time we should remember that life is a gamble
Each time is a journey because no one knows
What the future brings and holds
Yes we can try to plan and control our lives
But much to our dismay, we soon discover we can only do it
To a certain degree
If you can change things, do them better next time
Indeed, these are the realities of life

# Chapter IX

**Inspirational Messages**

### 1. Mother's Heart

A mother's heart is so strong
It can withstand all the pain
Sorrow and heartaches
Inflicted by loved ones
A mother's heart can still withstand
And forgives no matter what
Even there is no more left to give
One cannot fathom a heart of a mother
Unless you are a mother

## 2.

At times the anticipation

Of fear

Is even worse than

The reality itself

## 3.

Excuses will be made

Reasons will be given

But

To show how you

Care and love someone

You don't need excuses

It should

Be manifested in every way

### 4.

Be not deceived by

Those who easily weep and cry

By those who look kind and gentle

At times their hearts can be

As cold as ice

 **5.**

## What words failed to say

## The eyes say all

## 6.

When you gaze yourself at the mirror

Do you see the real you

Or just an illusion and impersonation

Of you

We have all the power to change

It all depends on you

## 7.

Just a simple smile

A warm hello and gracious thank you

Would make anyone's day

Very special

### 8.

One form of revenge

Is not hurting the opponents physically

It's about destroying them

Watching them fall apart

Mentally, emotionally and spiritually

It is even worse than a death sentence

## 9.

Friendship is like a business partnership

Both people should take responsibility

To nurture, work hard

To make it flourish and grow

## 10. Mothers

It's in the mother's heart

That children can find

Assurance of being loved

It's in the mother's arms

That children can find

Solace and comfort

But

It's in the mother's hugs and kisses

That the children can find the real joy

Of being loved and most of all

Being special and cared for

# My Wisdoms

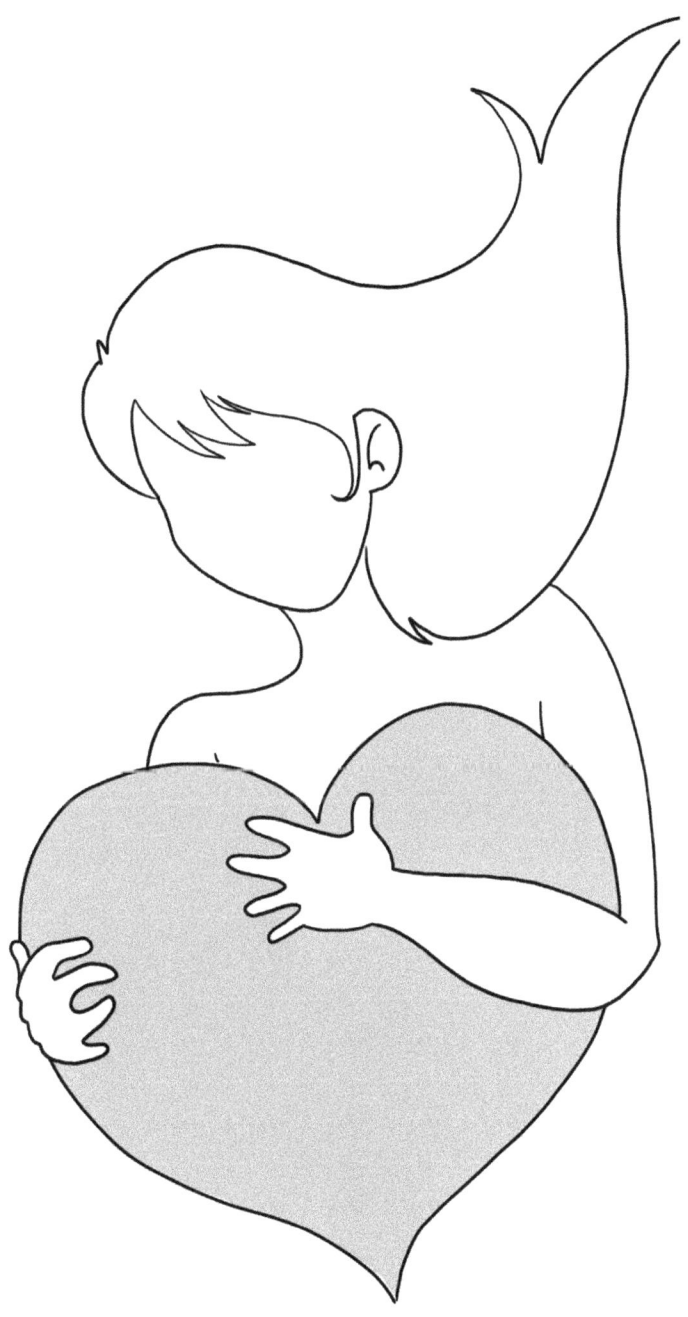

### 11. Love

A universal language

Love encompasses everything

Defies reasons, logic, and

Conquers all along its path

No one can be immune to

Its power, regardless of

Who you are

## 12.

We always mourn for

The loss of loved ones

But no one mourns

For the loss of one's soul

### 13.

There are times that it

Is vital

To analyse the past

Before

You can fathom or comprehend

The present and the future

## 14. Memories

It's a timeless remembrance

Of one's childhood, we all

Shared with friends and families

But then, change within us becomes

Inevitable and unavoidable

We start to drift apart

From all familiar faces, loved ones and friends

We begin to search for the quest of fame and

glory

Destroying everything that crosses our path

In order to achieve the success we so desire

Thus at the end upon reaching

The culmination of our success

We still feel miserable, lonely and empty

There is something void within our hearts

That no one can see

Only you can feel

You begin to question it

Is it all worth it?

To lose loved ones and friends

And most of all

Lose your soul?

It's not too late yet. You can change

And turn around your life

It's your choice, it's your decision

It's your life

## 15.

Your imagination is

The beginning and the stepping stones

For the creation and the

Fulfilment of your dream

## 16. I believe

As parents:

We make sure that our kids

Will be able to look after themselves

When we are gone

Teach them to be self-reliant

Independent

To be strong yet caring

To be focused, but aware of

Their own limitations

To be sensitive about different issues

Yet to be open minded to everything

We cannot be with them forever

And learning these values our

Kids will be equipped to face

All difficulties in life

## 17.

It is what we believe and our convictions

That make us who and what we are today

It is what we fight for that

Makes us stronger than ever

And most of all

It is our love and compassion

That can easily open our hearts

So we can help the people who need it most

## 18.

Reliving the moments

Of once beautiful memories

Can always bring

Sunshine and hope

Especially when one

Is in the middle

Of a personal conflict

### 19.

Though we are human
We still have the power to choose
To be evil and righteous
To be a success or be a failure
To be miserable or to be happy
To be moral or indecent
To be just or unjust
To be truthful or be deceitful
Whatever you choose
Will determine
Who and what you will be
Now and the future
You should be responsible
For your life
And no one else

## 20.

At times our ego

Is so much bigger and

Stronger than our conscience

Making us do the unthinkable

Making one's judgments unreasonable

Regardless of who will suffer

At the end

## 21.

Through the eyes of children

Their parents are their role models and their heroes

Therefore it is the responsibility

Of every parent to set high standards

To be able to produce

Future responsible adults.

## 22.

Being positive is one

Of the many ways

To face challenges in life

## 23.

Those who suffered abuse

Had pain and disappointments

In life

Will emerge either as

Stronger souls

Or people full of hatred of vengeance

At the end

Becoming the abusers and

Aggressors themselves

## 24.

When greed and envy overtake a person

Then you start selling your

Soul to the devil

And it's too late to realise

It is not all worth it

 **25.**

One should always be strong

To follow your beliefs and convictions

Failing to do so

Will haunt you forever

In your life

## 26. Change

Everything will come to an end

What was relevant before

Does not exist anymore

There will come a time when

You get tired of putting yourself

Last for others

It's time to embrace a new chapter

In your life.

And the only priority in mind

Is looking after oneself

First and foremost

Because nobody will do it for you

But yourself...a time for change

## 27.

Truth hurts, but then
Again, you cannot run
Forever from the truth

 **28.**

There are moments that the

Sweetest words to be heard

Are those that are yet unspoken

And still buried in one's heart

 **29.**

May one's life experiences

Be a pathway for perfection

Be an inspiration

To achieve your goals

And the ultimate dreams

Of your life

 **30.** 

Treating someone as a person first

Not by what and who they are

Or their status in the community

Nor what they can do for you

Is the noblest act of all

### 31.

Don't let your generosity

Be against you

At times people can

Manipulate and abuse, use you

For their own benefit

And satisfaction

### 32.

Perhaps the most agonising

Pain of all

Is the one still deep in your heart

That no one can see or tell

But you are the only one

That can feel and bear

### 33.

Honesty and being truthful

Begin first in oneself

Before it can fully

Transcend to others

Sounds simple but difficult to do

Especially when one's ego

Will be affected

## 34.

I wish I could be remembered

Not by whom I was

But by what I was

And the things I did

During my living years

### 35.

Some people judge you

For what they don't have

Or because of their own inadequacies

At times they rejoice for other's miseries

Abhor others for their

Achievement and success

An ugly side of human behavior

 **36.** 

People who pretend too much

Won't know when the fantasy ends

And the reality begins...

### 37.

At times we can learn

Something

From the innocence, purity,

And unadulterated mind

Of a child

### 38.

Ode to the lost loved one
Happiness and life together
We once had
Has been taken away from us
All those that we shared
Those precious moments
And precious times that we had
It's now just past memories
It's all that I have
They say time will heal
The pain I feel
But the scar and loneliness
In my heart
Will always be here
That will never take time to heal

## 39.

It's up to us to relinquish

The past

Then to let it go and move on

Failing to do so

We become a prisoner of ourselves

And peace within

Can never be found

## 40.

At times friends can ease

Sorrow and problems

They can be a guiding light

When you see yourself

Falling into pieces

When things go wrong

## 41.

There is no such thing

As one fits all in shoes

The same with people

Just because others did it

So well and succeeded

Does not mean you can

Do the same

## 42.

The first thoughts or words

That a person says

Will usually define

Their true character and personality

No matter the effort

Of how they want to change it

It is the subconscious mind

That dictates it

### 43. To a husband

Though the years pass
The stronger bond still exists
Both of us have changed physically
But we have grown stronger together
With a more mature outlook in life
Thus the love for one another
Continues to flow
Regardless of all obstacles
We have endured
As we walk
Through the journey
Of our lives
I am
Proud to have him as my husband
My soul mate
And my real best friend

## 44.

The impact or aftermath

We feel within

Is more significant

Than the experience

We had

Hence the next step

Will be crucial

And you can be the only one

Who can decide

On which road

Or journey of life to follow

### 45.

One of the reasons

We abhor others

Is because we can

See through them

Our inner weakness

That others don't have

## 46.

There are times

We want to leave

Away from our past

But our past never leaves us

Keeps on haunting us

Wherever and whenever we are

And it is up to us to accept

And deal with it courageously

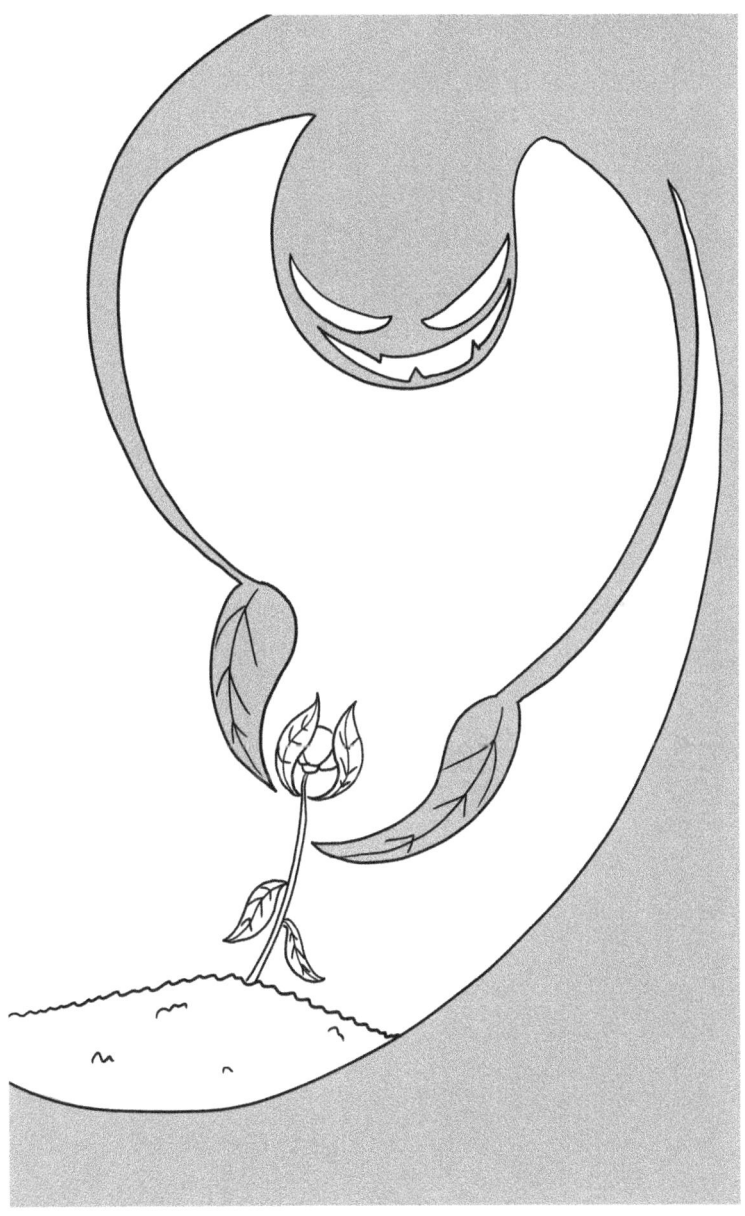

## 47.

What's wrong with today's world

No one wants to take responsibility

For their actions

Instead they opt for the easy way out

Blaming others

Except themselves

## 48.

Wondering what tomorrow brings

But anyway I just go on living

Until I reach my goal

Until I can be fully satisfied

That all my dreams will be fulfilled

## 49.

Once you can see through

The beauty, kindness, and greatness

Of each person

One's inner peace

Can be easily achieved

### 50. *I believe*

There is no right or wrong

It's just only a matter of opinion

Depends upon culture beliefs and convictions

—Lorna Ramirez

www.ingramcontent.com/pod-product-compliance
Lightning Source LLC
Chambersburg PA
CBHW051533010526
44107CB00064B/2715